SECURITIES INSTITUTE

S E R V I C E S

AN INTRODUCTION TO EQUITY MARKETS

PROFESSIONALISM | *INTEGRITY* | *EXCELLENCE*

AN INTRODUCTION TO EQUITY MARKETS

David Dasey

Second edition first published in 2002 in Great Britain by

Securities Institute (Services) Limited, Centurion House,

24 Monument Street, London EC3R 8AQ, England.

Written by David Dasey

ISBN: 1 84307 034 0

Second Edition, printed July 2002

First Edition printed August 1999

Printed and bound in Great Britain

by Antony Rowe Ltd, Chippenham, Wiltshire.

CONTENTS

About the Author

David is a Partner in The Professional Training Partnership, a UK training consultancy serving the securities industry and the legal and accountancy professions, and he has over 20 years training experience.

He has worked closely with the Securities Institute on the introduction of the 'International Capital Markets Qualifications' (ICMQ) into some of the Asian Markets and wrote the course workbooks for the 'Introduction to International Capital Markets' and 'International Equity Markets' papers of the ICMQ.

He has recently written the workbook for the Private Client Administration paper of the Securities Institute's Investment Administration Qualification.

David has over 10 years experience of preparing students for the UK Registered Representative exams (and similar compliance exams) and also for the Investment Analysis and Private Client Investment Advice papers of the Securities Institute Diploma. As well as ICMQ courses in Hong Kong and Shanghai he has also presented investment analysis courses in Tokyo, Seoul, Taipei, Kuala Lumpur, Bangkok, Johannesburg and Kiev.

David is a graduate of Imperial College, a Fellow of the Institute of Chartered Accountants in England and Wales and a Member of the Securities Institute.

Prior to joining the Professional Training Partnership he was Managing Director of the City Courses Division of, and a main board director of, the Financial Training Company.

Preface

The equities markets are huge business. The largest companies are valued at hundreds of billions of dollars; turnover in the markets is measured in terms of billions of dollars worth of shares daily. Investment in equities is no longer the preserve of the wealthy individual; the markets are readily accessible to all and with improving technology they are becoming increasingly more so. Shares are used as a home for long term savings, as a chance to have a punt and they underpin pension funds and life assurance policies.

The objective of this book is to provide an introduction to the equity market. It explains what shares are, the legal frame work within which they exist, how they are issued, how they are traded, how trades are settled, the effect of dividends, bonus issues and rights issues and an introduction to equity analysis.

This book is aimed at those who have little or no experience of the equity markets. It will be suitable for those starting work in securities and fund management firms and it provides useful background reading for those preparing for investment examinations. I also hope that the interested investor will also find the book useful in giving them an understanding of the mechanics of the markets.

ACKNOWLEDGMENTS
This book arose from an Introduction to Equity Markets course which I presented for the Securities Institute. I would like to thank Debra Wilson of the Institute for giving me the opportunity to write the book in the first place and for her encouragement along the way.

Chapter 1

WHAT ARE EQUITIES?

1.1 Introduction

The purpose of this chapter is to introduce you to companies, their shares and the markets. Many of the ideas introduced here are expanded upon in the following chapters. The chapter covers:

- The different types of business structure
- The features of companies
- The different types of companies
- The different types of share especially the equity share
- The reasons for investing in equities
- A brief history of the markets, particularly the London Stock Exchange

- An explanation of the Big Bang reforms of 1986
- The functions of the London Stock Exchange.

1.2 What is a company?

This introduction to equities starts with a review of the different structures that may be adopted by a business.

Goods and services are produced and sold by organisations, known as businesses, of which there are three main types:

i)   the sole trader or sole proprietorship
ii) the partnership, and
iii) the company.

The essential characteristics of *sole proprietorships* and *partnerships* are:

i)   the proprietor or partner is the owner of the business and also the manager;
ii) the business is formed with the minimum of regulation by, or registration with, regulatory authorities;
iii) capital is provided by the proprietor or partner or by borrowing; and
iv) the proprietor or partner has unlimited liability for the debts of the business; this means that if the business has liabilities greater than its assets (ie, it owes more in money terms than it owns) then those who are owed money by the business can obtain repayment from the private assets of the individual.

By contrast, a *company* is an organisation which allows investors to contribute capital, and thus become part–owners of the business, but not to have an unlimited liability for the debts of the business. In other words they have *limited liability*; if the company becomes insolvent then their investment may be worthless, but they will not be asked to contribute any more capital. These investors are called *shareholders* because they own shares in the company. Shareholders are also called *members* of the company.

Unlike the position in a sole proprietorship or a partnership, shareholders do not manage a company themselves. Instead they appoint other persons, who are called *directors,* to whom they delegate the task of management.

In many smaller, privately owned companies which have only a handful of shareholders, the shareholders simply appoint themselves as directors. Such companies are often called 'owner managed companies'. In large public companies there are thousands, or even hundreds of thousands, of shareholders. They appoint a board of usually between ten and twenty directors. Directors of public companies usually own shares in the companies but relative to the company an individual director's shareholding is not normally large.

A company is an organisation created by law and it is a separate legal entity from the people who currently own it, its shareholders. In the UK most companies are created, or *incorporated,* by registration with the Registrar of Companies – an official of the Department of Trade and Industry responsible for the registration of companies and maintaining the records of accounts and other statutory returns which companies are obliged to file.

The characteristics of a company may be summarised as follows:

i)   a company is a separate legal person from the persons who are its owners – the shareholders;

ii)   unlike a natural person who must eventually die, a company continues in existence indefinitely until it is terminated in the prescribed legal manner, although shareholders can, of course, transfer ownership of their shares;

iii)   a company owns its own property which cannot be appropriated by a shareholder;

iv)   a company can enter into contracts by which it is legally bound;

v)   the shareholders are not the managers of the company; the shareholders appoint directors to manage the company on their behalf;

vi)   a company is taxed separately from its shareholders; it is charged to corporation tax;

vii)   capital is provided by shareholders, through the issue of shares, or by borrowing, either from a bank or through the issue of bonds;

viii) shareholders have a limited liability for the debts the company – their liability being limited to the capital subscribed.

The term *stock* is sometimes used instead of share, particularly in the USA, and a company is sometimes described as a *joint–stock company*.

1.3 Types of company

1.3.1 METHOD OF INCORPORATION
Companies may be incorporated by

i)   Royal Charter – these are known as *chartered companies*. There are only a handful of these.
ii)   Separate Act of Parliament – these are called *statutory companies* – again there are relatively few of these.
iii)   Registration under the Companies Acts – these are called *registered companies*. Most companies are created in this way. There are over 1.5 million registered companies.

1.3.2 LIMITED LIABILITY COMPANIES
In a limited liability company the liability of the members of the company is limited. The limitation may be by shares or by guarantee.

Company limited by shares
The liability of the members is limited to the amount, if any, unpaid on the shares. Once the shares are fully paid up there is, in general, no further liability. Most companies are companies limited by shares.

Fully paid up means that the issue price of the shares, when they were first issued, has been paid in full to the company. When shares are first issued the issue price is normally paid in full. Sometimes, however, shares may be issued where the issue price is paid in instalments. Until such time as the issue price is paid in full the shares are described as partly paid and shareholders can be called on to pay the outstanding amount of the share price. Shares traded on the Stock Exchange can be assumed to be fully paid unless they are described as 'partly paid'.

Company limited by guarantee

In a company limited by guarantee, the liability of shareholders is limited to the amount they undertake to contribute in the event of winding up. If the company is wound up, each member at the time of the winding up or within one year of the winding up may be required to contribute up to the amount of his guarantee towards the debts incurred while he was a member. The amounts are usually very small, eg £1. Most such companies are associations or institutions; for example, the Securities Institute is a company limited by guarantee.

Unlimited liability companies

In addition to limited liability companies there are also some *unlimited liability companies* where there is no limit to the liability of members to contribute to the debts of the company if it is wound up. Such companies may be used if a corporate structure is required but limited liability is unimportant. Unlimited liability companies are not covered in this book.

1.3.3 PLC OR PRIVATE (LTD)

The main difference between private companies (which have 'limited' or 'ltd' at the end of their name) and public limited companies (plcs) is the ability of plcs to offer shares to the public. A private company cannot raise capital by offering shares to the public.

A public limited company is a company which is registered as such and must comply with the following requirements:

i)   It must state that it is a public limited company both in its memorandum of association and in its name. The memorandum of association must contain a clause stating that it is a public limited company and the name must end with "Public Limited Company" or "PLC" (The memorandum of association is described in Chapter 2, paragraph 2.8)

ii)   The memorandum of association must be in the form specified in Table F of the Companies (Table A to F) Regulations 1985.

iii) It must have an authorised share capital of at least £50,000.

iv)   Before it can commence business, it must have allotted shares to the value of at least £50,000. Each share allotted must be paid up to at least one quarter of its nominal value together with the whole of any premium. (eg a share of 25p sold for £1.50 has a premium of £1.25 which must be paid together with 6.25p as one quarter of the nominal value. Total £1–31.25p. At least 200,000 of these shares would have to be allotted).

1.4 Sources of capital for a company

As noted above a company obtains its capital in two ways:

- from shareholders, *or*
- by borrowing.

Shareholders contribute capital in exchange for shares. A *share* gives an entitlement to a share in profits. Shares in companies can be bought and sold and thus over time, the ownership of the company will change.

Traditionally companies have borrowed money from banks. However, companies can borrow directly from investors and issue to an investor a *certificate* which acknowledges the loan, and which promises to pay interest, usually at a fixed rate, and repay the capital at a stated future date. Such a certificate is called a *bond*. When a bond reaches the end of its term and it is said to have matured and the repayment of capital is called *redemption*. The investor can hold the bond until *maturity* or he can sell the bond onto another person.

1.5 Types of shares

All companies will have *ordinary shares* and some companies will also have *preference shares* and possibly *deferred shares*.

1.5.1 ORDINARY SHARES

Every company has *ordinary shares*. The ordinary shareholders are the true owners of the company. They are entitled to the balance of the income of the company after all prior charges have been paid and if the company goes into a liquidation, the ordinary shareholders are entitled to the balance of the assets after all debts have been repaid. The entitlement to the balance of the income and the assets of a company is called the *equity* of the company. Consequently, ordinary shares are also called *equity shares* or *equities*.

In the USA ordinary shares are called *common* stock.

1.5.2 PREFERENCE SHARES

Some companies issue another class of share, the *preference share*, which is entitled to a dividend in priority to, or in preference to, the equity shares. In a liquidation the shares are entitled to repayment in priority to the equity shares. Preference shares are also called *preferred shares* or *preferred stock*.

1.5.3 DEFERRED SHARES

A rarer class of share is the *deferred share*, the holder of which is only entitled to a dividend if the ordinary shareholders have been paid a specified minimum dividend. If the specified minimum is not paid to the ordinary shareholder then the deferred shareholder gets nothing.

1.6 Why invest in shares?

A person chooses to invest their money on the basis of the return that they will receive. They judge the return in the light of the risks associated with that investment.

A shareholder has the right to share in the profits of the company. Each year the company will, hopefully, make profits and it pays out part of this profit to the shareholders as a cash payment. This payment is called a *dividend*. The amount of dividend depends on the level of profits, and if profits increase from one year to the next, then so should the dividend. Shares therefore offer the possibility of an increasing income, or *income growth*, to the investor; but there is a risk. If the profits fall then so will the dividend and if the company makes a loss, then it may not be able to pay a dividend at all.

Over time the company hopes to grow. It will increase in size and make larger profits. The value of the shares will also grow and the shareholder can sell their shares at a profit. Thus shares offer the prospect of *capital growth*. The disadvantage is that shares can fall in value and if the company fails and becomes insolvent, the shares will become worthless.

Investors therefore invest in shares for:

* income and growth in that income, and
* growth in the value of their shares – capital growth.

1.7 Sources of share capital

Share capital may be raised from

i)   the original founders of the company
ii)   private investors
iii) other companies
iv)   investing institutions such as pension funds, life assurance companies, unit trusts and investment trusts
v)   venture capital investors such as banks, specialist investment trusts and venture capital trusts.

1.8 A brief history of the markets

Modern joint stock companies and stock markets first developed in the seventeenth and eighteenth centuries in the great international trading countries like England and Holland. An entrepreneur wishing to undertake a trading expedition to the newly discovered parts of the world such as the East Indies and the West Indies would create a joint stock company whereby investors would provide risk capital in exchange for a share in the profits of the venture. The first company was The Muscovy Company, established in 1553. Other famous companies created in the seventeenth century include the Hudson Bay Company and the East India Company. Dealing in the shares of these and other companies started, at first, informally but eventually organised exchanges were formed. It is no surprise that the earliest exchanges were Amsterdam and London as Britain and Holland established their trading empires. The London Stock Exchange was formally established in 1773.

The opening up of North America to European traders and settlers also led to the creation of joint stock companies and the New York Stock Exchange started in 1792.

The industrial revolution in Europe and the development of the USA in the eighteenth and nineteenth centuries saw an ever increasing demand for capital by industrialists and traders who used the stock exchanges to raise their funds. Thus the stock markets in the industrialised western countries grew.

The last 50 years, and particularly the last 20-25 years, have seen the world wide spread of western style businesses and the subsequent development of stock exchanges in many countries.

1.9 A brief history of the London Stock Exchange

1553	First joint stock company created
1694	Bank of England created and the first 'gilts' (British government bonds) issued
1760	After being ejected from the Royal Exchange because of unruly behaviour stockbrokers start meeting at Jonathon's coffee house

1773	Brokers at Jonathon's create The Stock Exchange
1801	Foundation Stone laid on the present site. By the end of the nineteenth century there were over 20 stock exchanges in cities throughout the UK.
1908	Single capacity and fixed commissions introduced. Single capacity meant that firms could be either brokers or jobbers (market makers) but not both.
1973	Regional Exchanges merge to form one exchange
1986	Big Bang – major reforms of the London Stock Exchange which resulted in the exchange structure in place today.
1995	AIM, a market for smaller companies, is launched.
1997	Settlement services are transferred to CREST. Share certificates replaced by accounts in a computer system.
	SETS – electronic order book – a new system for dealing in shares.
2000	The exchange becomes a public limited company, The London Stock Exchange plc.
	The exchange's role as the UK Listing Authority is transferred to the Financial Services Authority.

2001   The London Stock Exchange plc becomes a
       listed company.

The most recent development, and an extremely important one for the future, was the announcement in July 1998 by the London Stock Exchange and Frankfurt's Deutsche Börse of the formation of a strategic alliance, with the aim of harmonising the markets for leading UK and German securities and developing a joint electronic trading platform.

The first phase of the Alliance went live at the start of January 1999, providing a common access package for both exchanges and a single point of liquidity for UK and German stocks. This is hoped to be the first step on the road to the creation of a pan–European market for blue chip shares. Several other European exchanges have subsequently indicated their wish to participate.

1.10 Big Bang 1986

In the late 1970's the London Stock Exchange started to come under pressure to reform its structure and practices. Pressure came from two sources:

i) from the government in respect of the Exchange's rule book which was deemed to contravene the restrictive practices legislation. The government decided to take the Exchange to the Restrictive Practices Court;

ii)   from commercial pressures: exchange member firms were largely UK owned partnerships – the individual partners being members of the exchange. The abolition of exchange controls in 1979 enabled UK investors to invest more easily overseas and the UK firms faced competition from overseas brokers for this business. The overseas brokers also wanted to deal in the shares of UK companies. By comparison with the overseas brokers the UK firms were small and lacked the capacity to deal in size.

In response to the threatened court action the Exchange agreed an out of court settlement with the government to reform its structure and rules.

The changes thus brought about were referred to as *Big Bang*.

The principal changes were:

i)   Outside ownership of members firms was permitted and a firm could be owned by a single outside corporation. Many firms were bought by UK and overseas banks and overseas securities firms.

ii)   Membership and voting rights were moved from individual members to corporate members

iii)   Minimum scales of commissions were abolished

iv)   Single capacity was abolished. All firms became 'broker /dealers' meaning that they had the capacity to act as agency brokers and also to register as market makers buying and selling on their own account.

v)   A further change was the introduction of a new computer system, SEAQ, to operate alongside the Exchange trading floor. SEAQ was so successful that the floor was abandoned after just a few weeks.

1.11 Functions of the London Stock Exchange

The London Stock Exchange is a Recognised Investment Exchange under the Financial Services Act 1986 and it is regulated by the Financial Services Authority.

The London Stock Exchange serves two purposes:

i)   To provide a mechanism for companies and governments to issue new securities in order to raise money. This function is known as the *primary market.*

ii)   To provide a means for investors to buy and sell securities that have already been issued. This function is known as the *secondary market.*

The Exchange's secondary market operations are carried out through six secondary markets:

i)   the domestic equity market – UK listed companies
ii)   the Alternative Investment Market (AIM)
iii) the international equity market – non–UK companies
iv)   the gilt and fixed interest market

v)   the covered warrants market

vi)   the traditional options market.

1.12 International comparisons

Statistics published by the World Federation of Exchanges give the following details for domestic equity markets at 31 December 2001:

	Market Capitalisation £m	Number of listed companies
New York	11,026,586	1,939
NASDAQ	2,739,674	3,618
Tokyo	2,264,527	2,103
London	2,164,716	1,923
Euronext	1,843,528	1,132
Deutsche Borse	1,071,748	748

The *market capitalisation* of a company means the market price per share multiplied by the number of shares in issue. For example a company which has 100 million shares in issue with a share price of 200p per share will have a market capitalisation of £200 million (100 million shares x £2 per share). The market capitalisation of a stock market is the sum of the market capitalisations of all the companies listed on the exchange.

Chapter 2

SHAREHOLDERS AND COMPANY LAW

2.1 Introduction

In this chapter some of the legal framework for companies is explained. Companies are artificial beings and the rights and responsibilities of the company and those persons associated with it must be laid down in law. The chapter looks at:

* The meaning of a share
* The Companies Acts
* Shareholders rights

- Nominal value
- Registered shares and nominees
- Dividends
- The company's constitution
- Directors and corporate governance
- Company meetings
- Preference shares.

2.2 The meaning of a share

In the previous chapter a share was described as representing an owner's share in a company and as giving an entitlement to profits. But what exactly is a share? A useful description is that a share is the interest of a shareholder in a company, the company's capital being divided into a number of equal shares. This interest of a shareholder is represented by a number of shareholders rights, one of which is the right to participate in the profits of the company.

Before we look in more detail at shareholders rights there are two important points to make:

i) although a shareholder is a part owner of a company he does not own any of the company's assets; the company as a separate legal entity owns its own assets itself;

ii) a share is not the same as a share certificate; a certificate is merely evidence of title to the shares.

2.3 Company Law

The legal framework for companies is provided by the Companies Acts 1985 and 1989. The 1985 act is the major act, being a consolidation of the previous acts; the 1989 act made additions and amendments to the 1985 act.

Although 1985 may sound quite modern, much company law has its roots in the mid–19th century and some areas are looking distinctly old fashioned. A steering group was appointed by the Department of Trade and Industry in 1998 to carry out a long term review of company law. It published its final report in July 2001 recommending some fundamental reforms. The government will be consulting on draft legislation when it has had an opportunity to analyse the report. We can therefore expect to see another companies act in the next few years. This development is much welcomed by practitioners.

2.4 Shareholders Rights

A share can be regarded as a collection of rights granted to the shareholder by the Companies Acts and the company's memorandum and articles of association.

The main rights of the shareholder are

i)   to receive notices of all meetings of the company
ii)   to attend, speak and vote at such meetings

iii) to appoint a proxy to attend and vote at the meeting on their behalf

iv) to share in the profits of the company; profits are distributed to shareholders as dividends, each share being entitled to an equal dividend, unless they are preference shares or deferred shares

v) to receive the annual report and accounts of the company at least 21 days prior to the Annual General Meeting

vi) to vote to appoint and remove directors

vii) to vote to appoint the auditors

viii) to receive a bonus issue on a pro–rata basis

ix) to be offered shares in a rights issue on a pro–rata basis – this is known as the shareholders' *pre–emptive rights*

x) to sell/ transfer shares without restriction

xi) to share in the assets of the company if the company goes into liquidation – in a liquidation (or winding up) of a company the shareholders vote to bring the company to an end; the debts of the company are paid off and the remaining assets are sold with the proceeds being distributed to the shareholders

xii) to be consulted in the event of specified circumstances, for example if the company is proposing a particularly large acquisition.

2.5 Nominal Value

Shares may be issued with or without a nominal value. *Nominal value* is also known as *par value* or face value and it represents the minimum price at which a share can be issued. All UK company shares have a nominal value because UK company legislation does not permit shares of no par value. Both the USA and Japan allow no par value shares, although the majority of shares do have a par value. The nominal value is usually of little significance and should not be confused with the market value of the share.

When shares are issued they may be issued at the nominal value but it is very common for the shares to be issued at a higher price. For example, a share with a nominal value of 25p might be issued for 150p. 25p is the nominal value and the additional 125p is called the *share premium* and it will be disclosed separately in the company's accounts.

Company law prohibits the issue of shares at less than nominal value.

2.6 Evidence of ownership

Shares may be issued as *registered shares* or as *bearer shares*. Most UK company shares are issued as registered shares.

2.6.1 REGISTERED SHARES

A register is a record, maintained by the company issuing shares, of the current holders of those shares. A share where ownership is recorded on a register is called a *registered share*.

The official of the company responsible for maintaining the register of its shareholders is called the *registrar*. Although the company has the legal responsibility for maintaining the register, in many cases they employ a specialist registrar company to perform the task for them.

In law the legal owner of a share is the person whose name appears on the register of members (shareholders).

Evidence of the entry of a name in the register may be provided by either

- a share certificate, or
- a stock account within CREST.

A *share certificate* is a document provided by the company to the shareholder certifying details of ownership. A registered certificate includes a statement with words to the effect that the person named on the certificate is the registered holder of the shares concerned.

Certificates are important documents and investors must take care of them. The loss of a certificate causes much administrative, and possible legal, difficulty and many investors who hold certificates themselves actually keep them in a secure place, such as at their bank.

CREST is the shareholding and transfer system which allows for shares to held in computer accounts within the CREST system. Shares held within CREST are not evidenced by a certificate and the shares are sometimes described as being de–materialised.

2.6.2 REGISTERED NAMES

A share may be registered:

- in the name of the actual owner, who is sometimes called the *beneficial owner* of the share, or
- in the name of a *nominee.*

If the share is registered in the name of the beneficial owner that person will either:

- be a member, or a sponsored member, of CREST, or
- hold a share certificate.

Membership and sponsored membership of CREST are explained in Chapter 5.

2.6.3 NOMINEES

Many investors find it convenient for their investments to be held by someone else on their behalf. This other person is called a *nominee.*

For example, if a private investor's portfolio is being managed by a firm of brokers then it will be administratively easier for the shares to be registered in the name of the broking firm's nominee company on behalf of the client.

Proper regulations need to be in place to ensure that such nominee holdings are properly accounted for by the firm and to safeguard the investor's position. Financial Services Authority regulations require that the firm has a separate nominee company to hold clients' investments, thus ensuring that the clients' investments are kept separate from those owned by the firm itself.

Nominee accounts can be either

- 'pooled,' or
- 'designated'.

In both cases the broker registers the shares in the name of the nominee company.

If the accounts are pooled, the broker maintains just one registration for any particular company and records all the clients' holdings under that one registration.

If the accounts are designated, then each person's holding is registered separately, still in the nominee company's name but with an additional identifying code.

An investor should consider the following matters before using a nominee:

- Receipt of annual report and accounts – will the nominee arrange for the beneficial owner to receive the annual report and accounts and, if so, will a charge be made?
- Attendance at AGMs – will the nominee arrange for the beneficial owner to attend the Annual General Meeting and other meetings of the company and, if so, will a charge be made?

- Timing of dividend receipts – dividends are paid by the company to the nominee; are they paid on to the beneficial owner straight away?
- Shareholder perks – will the beneficial owner be entitled to shareholder perks such as discounts on the company's goods and services? Often these are lost if the shares are held by a nominee.
- Charges – what charges does the broker make for the nominee facility?
- Security – is the shareholder satisfied that their shares are held securely and cannot be misallocated either to the firm or to another client of the firm?

2.6.4 CHANGE OF OWNERSHIP

When registered shares are transferred from one person to another it is necessary for the share register to be altered to record the change of ownership, deleting the name of the old owner and recording the name of the new owner.

The process of transfer of ownership is regulated by legislation.

If the issue is in certificated form then the old certificate needs to be cancelled and a new one issued in the name of the new owner.

For shares held in CREST there are no physical certificates to be moved about. Transfer is effected by making the necessary changes to the computer records.

Where transfer of a security is effected simply by altering computer records, with no movement of certificates, it is described as a *book entry transfer system*.

In some markets, but not in the UK, it is common for securities to be held not by the actual owner nor by their nominee, but in a *central depository* which holds securities on behalf of investors. The depository has safe custody of the certificates and it will maintain its own record of the true underlying owner. When there is a change of ownership the depository simply alters its records – book entry transfer again.

The depository collects dividends and pays them on to the beneficial owner.

Shares held in a depository are said to be *immobilised* as opposed to shares held on computer, such as within CREST which are said to be *de-materialised*.

2.6.5 BEARER SHARES

With a *bearer share* the company does not maintain a register and therefore ownership involves physical possession of a certificate.

A bearer certificate contains a statement that the bearer, or holder, of the certificate is the legal owner of the share.

Change of ownership simply means the transfer of the certificate from the old owner to the new owner. There is no register to be altered.

Bearer shares are far less common than registered shares but many bonds are issued in bearer form.

2.7 Dividends

2.7.1 DISTRIBUTABLE PROFITS

A dividend is a payment to shareholders out of the profits of the company. To ensure that the assets of a company are not depleted at the expense of the creditors, company law restricts the type of profit which can be distributed to shareholders. Profits and losses can be divided into two types: realised and unrealised.

A *realised profit* is one which has arisen from a real transaction. For example, if a company sells an asset then it will make, or realise, a profit or a loss on the transaction. An unrealised profit is one which arises simply because the asset has increased in value but has not been sold. For example a company may buy a building for £1 million; three years later the building may be worth £1.6 million. The company may recognise the increase in value in its accounts but the profit of £0.6 million is unrealised: it has not arisen from a sale. An unrealised profit is sometimes referred to as a book profit.

Realised profits can be distributed as a dividend but unrealised profits can not be distributed.

2.7.2 INTERIM AND FINAL DIVIDENDS

The frequency with which companies pay dividends varies: some companies pay one dividend a year, some pay two dividends a year and some pay four dividends. If more than one dividend is paid then the earlier dividend(s) are called *interim dividends* and the last dividend is called a *final dividend*. More detail on dividends is given in Chapter 8.

2.8 Company Constitution

The constitution of a company is contained in two documents – the Memorandum of Association and the Articles of Association.

2.8.1 MEMORANDUM OF ASSOCIATION

The memorandum of association sets out the relationship of the company with the outside world and it contains the following clauses:

i)   Name of the company
ii) Domicile (registered office)
iii) Authorised share capital – the maximum share capital that the company is allowed to issue
iv) Statement that the liability of the shareholders is limited
v)   Objects – what the company is allowed to do
vi) Whether the company is a public limited company.

2.8.2 ARTICLES OF ASSOCIATION

The articles of association are a contract between the company and the shareholders and will provide regulations in the following areas:

i)   Shareholders rights
ii) Borrowing powers
iii) Dividends
iv) Meetings
v)   Directors
vi) Winding up.

2.9 Directors

The directors are appointed by the shareholders to manage the company. A distinction is often made between *executive directors* and *non executive directors*. An executive director means one with an operational responsibility within the company.

Non–executive directors have an important role to play in the running of a company because they can bring independent judgement and outside experience and expertise to the Board's deliberations and can act as a form of overseer for the executive directors.

There have been three reports in recent years on the question of corporate governance and directors – the Cadbury Report, the Greenbury Report and the Hampel Report.

2.9.1 THE CADBURY REPORT – 1992

The Cadbury committee (chaired by Sir Adrian Cadbury) issued a Code of Best Practice. The main recommendations were:

i)   Listed companies to have at least 3 non–executives

ii)   The positions of Chairman and Chief Executive to be held by separate persons

iii) Board meetings to held regularly and have a proper agenda of matters specifically reserved to the Board for decision.

iv)   An audit committee of non–executive directors to be formed to consider matters relating to internal and external audit and to evaluate the integrity and standards of internal controls and financial reporting.

2.9.2 THE GREENBURY REPORT – 1995

The Greenbury committee (chaired by Sir Richard Greenbury) made four main recommendations with regard to director's remuneration:

i)   there should be a remuneration committee comprising the non–executive directors

ii)   the remuneration committee should determine the remuneration of the executive directors

iii) to ensure the integrity of the remuneration committee there should be no cross directorships

iv)   directors' service contracts should be limited to one year.

2.9.3 THE HAMPEL COMMITTEE – 1998

The Hampel Committee (chaired by Sir Ronald Hampel) reviewed Cadbury and Greenbury and published a Combined Code comprising Principles of Good Governance and Code of Best Practice. It replaces the Cadbury and Greenbury Codes. It retains much of Cadbury and Greenbury but makes some changes and enhancements in the light of the experience of operating Cadbury and Greenbury.

The Combined Code is mandatory for all listed companies.

2.10 Company Meetings

There are two types of meeting:

i)   Annual General Meeting (AGM)
ii)   Extra–ordinary General Meeting (EGM).

2.10.1. ANNUAL GENERAL MEETING (AGM)

At least 21 days notice is needed and the ordinary business decided at the meeting includes:

i)   Approve the accounts – these will have been sent to shareholders with the notice of the meeting.
ii)   Vote on the dividend proposed by the directors.
iii)   Appoint directors to fill vacancies and re–appoint directors whose term of office has ended and who are standing for re–election.
iv)   Appoint auditors for the coming year.

In addition to the ordinary business there may special business such as:

i)   the issue of further shares
ii)   approve share buybacks
iii)   change the constitution
iv)   approve waiver of pre–emptive rights.

The shareholder has the right to attend, speak and vote at the meeting. The shareholder may appoint a *proxy* to attend on their behalf and to cast their votes. The proxy is an individual appointed by the shareholder to act on their behalf. Usually the shareholder appoints one of the directors to act as proxy, but it does not have to be a director; any person may be appointed as a proxy. The proxy casts the shareholder's votes in accordance with the instructions of the shareholder.

At meetings shareholders are asked to vote on resolutions:

i)   Ordinary resolutions which require over a 50% majority
ii)   Special resolutions which require a 75% majority. Special resolutions are relatively rare. Most business is decided by ordinary resolutions. Examples of special resolution would be the disapplication of pre–emption rights or the winding up of the company.

2.10.2 EXTRA–ORDINARY GENERAL MEETING (EGM)

If it is necessary to call the shareholders together between AGMs then an extraordinary general meeting is called. Meetings are usually called by the company but an EGM can be requisitioned by 10% of shareholders.

2.11 Preference Shares

A preference share is one which gives the holder a preference over ordinary shares in two respects: dividend payments and payment in a winding up.

The features of preference shares are:

i)   the dividend is a fixed amount per share – preference shares do not offer the income growth prospects of ordinary shares;

ii) in a winding up, or on earlier redemption, the shares are repaid only at their nominal value – there is no prospect of long term capital growth; and

iii) preference shares usually have no, or at best only limited, voting rights.

2.11.1 PREFERENCE IN RESPECT OF DIVIDENDS

If a company decides to pay a dividend in a year then it must pay the preference dividend even if it decides not to pay an ordinary dividend. It cannot ignore the preference shares and pay a dividend only to the ordinary shares. However, if the company decides not to pay a dividend at all, because for example it has made losses, then the preference shareholders will have no right of action against the company.

Preference shares may be *cumulative preference shares* or *non–cumulative preference shares*. The distinction becomes important if the company fails to pay a preference dividend. With a cumulative preference share the entitlement to the dividend accumulates and the arrears of preference dividend must be paid before any ordinary dividend. There is no accumulation with a non–cumulative preference share where a missed dividend is simply lost.

2.11.2 PREFERENCE IN A WINDING UP

In the liquidation or winding up of a company the order in which the various persons owed money by the company are repaid is laid down in company law. The order of priority is:

1. Loans and bonds secured on assets of the company by a fixed charge – a charge over a specific asset or assets of the company.
2. Preferential creditors eg unpaid taxes and unpaid wages.
3. Loans and bonds secured on assets of the company by a floating charge – a charges over the assets of the company generally, excluding any assets covered by a fixed charge.
4. Unsecured loans and bonds and other unsecured creditors (a creditor is a person who is owed money by the company)
5. Subordinated loan stocks – these are a special type of loan stock which rank after the unsecured creditors but before shareholders
6. Preference shares
7. Ordinary shares.

Thus preference shares are repaid before the ordinary shares but after all other creditors.

Chapter 3

ISSUING SHARES – THE PRIMARY MARKET

3.1 Introduction

In this chapter the primary market – the issuing of shares – is explained.

The chapter starts with an explanation of flotation:

- What is meant by a flotation
- Why companies float
- Where they are floated
- When they are floated and
- The role of the sponsor.

The chapter then goes on to look at:

- The requirements for a company to obtain a full listing in the UK
- The contents of the listing particulars or prospectus
- The requirements for admission to the Alternative Investment Market
- Flotation methods

And the chapter finishes with a few ideas about:

- The issue price.

3.2 Flotation

The process of bringing a company's shares to the market for the first time is called a *flotation* or *stock market flotation*.

Floating a company entails either:

- applying for a *listing* of the shares on the main market of a stock exchange; or

- satisfying the requirements of a junior market which will be less demanding than those for a full listing.

A company applying for a full listing on the main market of an exchange must satisfy certain minimum criteria with respect to:

- Size of the company
- Number of shares to be offered to investors
- Period of profitable trading
- Integrity and experience of the directors.

An application for listing is made to the authority designated for that purpose by the legislation of the country concerned. For example, in the UK the Financial Services Authority regulates listing.

The rationale behind having formal listing requirements is that the Exchange wants only shares in companies that have some substance and where there is a wide spread of shareholders thus ensuring an active secondary market. Furthermore, investors want confidence that companies who offer shares to the public have complied with formal disclosure requirements and that the company and all the documentation has been scrutinised.

3.3 Second Tier Markets

In addition to having a listed market some exchanges have a second tier market for companies which cannot meet the requirements for listing. Examples of second tier markets are the Alternative Investment Market (AIM) of the London Stock Exchange and the Second Section of the Tokyo Stock Exchange.

Companies whose shares are dealt on a second tier market are usually smaller and often newer companies than listed companies. If a second tier company eventually meets the requirements for listing then it can apply for a full listing. A promotion to the main list is not automatic; it has to be applied for.

3.4 Why float a company?

A company may be floated for one or more of the following reasons:

- *To raise finance for the company.*
  When new shares are issued in a flotation the sale proceeds provide cash (new finance) for the company.

- *To allow the existing owners to sell some or all of their shares.*
  As part of the flotation process the existing shareholders of the company have the opportunity to sell some or all of their shares thus realising their investment in the company.

  An alternative to a flotation for this reason would be to arrange a private sale of the company.

- *To privatise a company previously under State control.*
  Over the last 15 to 20 years many governments have decided to sell into private hands enterprises previously owned by the government. This is done for a variety of reasons, the main ones being firstly, a political belief that such businesses should be owned privately rather than be State controlled and secondly, the sale raises money for the government.

  A company may be privatised by floating it on the stock exchange.

- *To demerge part of a company by floating it as a separate company*

3.5 Where to float?

Having decided to float the company the owners must now consider where to float. The choices available are:

- To float on the single exchange of the country of residence.

  Clearly if there is only one exchange in a country then the company must float on that exchange.

- To float on the junior market instead of the main market.

If a company does not satisfy the listing requirements then the junior market (if there is one) is the only choice. However companies which do satisfy the listing rules may choose to join a junior market because of lower costs, or less regulation, or perhaps different tax treatment of the shareholders.

- There may be more than one exchange in a country and if so a choice must be made as to which one to float.

  For example in the USA there are several stock exchanges and a company will decide which one to join.

- To float on an overseas exchange rather than the domestic exchange.

  A company may choose this route if perhaps the home market is small and illiquid or perhaps the company, although based in its home country, carries on most of its business overseas. (Liquidity means the ease with which the shares may be bought and sold)

- To float on both the domestic exchange and an overseas exchange.

  Large companies may list in more than one country in order to attract overseas investors and to improve the liquidity of the shares world–wide.

3.6 When to float?

Generally a company will try to float at a time when the market is buoyant and thus the company and the existing shareholders raise as much money as possible. In the case of privatisations political expediency will be an important factor.

Investor sentiment is also important and sometimes investors can turn against new issues. This is especially so at times of falling prices or when there have been a large number of flotations when a 'flotation fatigue' sets in.

3.7 How to float?

Having decided to float a company the directors must then employ a 'sponsor' to advise them and lead them through the flotation process. The sponsor will be a merchant bank or a stock-broking firm or the corporate finance department of a firm of accountants.

The sponsor will:

- Advise on which exchange to apply for listing
- Advise on the size and method of flotation
- Advise on the share price for the flotation
- Prepare the listing particulars for submission to the authorities and subsequent issue to potential investors
- Advertise the sale and handle all the applications for shares

- Arrange for the issue to be underwritten. Underwriting means paying a small commission to banks and other institutional investors to take up any shares which are not applied for in the flotation.
- Generally assist the company in its flotation.

In this work the sponsor will use other specialists such firms of lawyers and reporting accountants.

3.8 New issues

Share issues can be divided into two categories:

i) *Primary issues* – a primary issue is an issue of shares when a company is first admitted to an exchange. Such an issue is also called an '*Initial Public Offer*' or IPO.

ii) *Secondary issues* – a secondary issue is an issue of new shares by a company which is already listed; examples are rights issues and scrip issues.

Do not confuse the terms primary issue and secondary issue with primary market and secondary market.

3.9 The Competent Authority for Listing - the UK Listing Authority

The Competent Authority for Listing is the government agency responsible for making the Listing Rules, which lay down the requirements which issuers of securities to the UK primary markets need to meet, and for policing compliance with these Rules. It is also responsible for admitting securities to the UK's Official List.

Under EU regulation each member state must appoint a competent authority. The Competent Authority for Listing is the Financial Services Authority. In this capacity the FSA is called the UK Listing Authority (UKLA).

Responsibility for the Competent Authority for Listing transferred from the London Stock Exchange to the Financial Services Authority on 1 May 2000. This transfer of responsibility follows the London Stock Exchange's proposal to demutualise and turn itself into a commercial company.

3.10 The UKLA and the London Stock Exchange

With the transfer of the UKLA to the FSA a flotation in the UK now requires two applications:

(i)   To the UKLA for admission to the Official List and

(ii)   To the London Stock Exchange for admission to trading

These two applications are linked: shares will not be admitted to the Official List unless they are also admitted to trading and shares will not be admitted to trading unless they are also admitted to the Official List.

3.11 Admission to Listing

To be admitted to the Official List securities must satisfy the requirements of the Listing Rules. These rules are contained in a binder with a purplish cover and consequently the rules are referred to simply as the 'Purple Book'.

The principal requirements for listing are:

* The market value of the securities must be at least £700,000 for shares and £200,000 other debt securities.
* The securities must be freely transferable.

- At least 25% of any class of shares must be in the hands of the public (ie, persons not associated with the directors or major shareholders).
- The company must have been trading for at least three years; the UKLA however may waive this condition.
- The issue of warrants or options to subscribe equity must be limited to 20% of the issued equity at the time of issue of the options or warrants.
- The listing particulars must contain three years audited accounts ending not more than six months before the date of the listing particulars.
- The securities must be eligible for electronic settlement.
- The directors must have appropriate expertise and experience for managing the business.

As part of the admission to listing companies agree to comply with the *continuing obligations* of the Listing Rules. These include amongst other things:

- Making all price sensitive announcements through a Regulatory Information Service.
- Making all dividend announcements through a Regulatory Information Service.
- Publishing full year accounts within 6 months of the year end date.
- Publishing $1/2$ year results within 90 days of the half year date.
- Giving additional detailed information in the annual accounts.

A Regulatory Information Service is a service, approved by the UKLA, that receives regulatory information from listed companies (and other entities), processes that information and circulates it to Secondary Information Providers. There are seven Regulatory Information Services.

There are approximately 1,800 UK companies and approximately 500 overseas companies admitted to the Official List.

3.12 Listing Particulars

A new issue of shares will be made according to the law of the country concerned and usually the company will have to prepare and make public a document known as the *listing particulars* or *prospectus*.

The listing particulars is a formal document that will give all relevant details of:

- The company and its capital
- The persons responsible for the prospectus
- The shares on offer
- The business activities of the company and its subsidiaries
- The directors of the company
- Financial details including the audited accounts for the past three years
- Recent developments
- Profits forecasts
- Reasons for making the issue.

The listing particulars comprise a lengthy document full of a lot of technical detail that the prospective investor will analyse in order to decide whether to subscribe for the issue or not. There is a considerable responsibility on the directors and the professional advisors to the company to ensure that the factual information in the prospectus is correct.

3.13 Trading on the London Stock Exchange

Shares issued and/or dealt on the London Stock Exchange must be either:

* Admitted to the Official List; or
* Admitted to the Alternative Investment Market

3.14 Alternative Investment Market

In 1980 the London Stock Exchange introduced the Unlisted Securities Market (USM) as a mechanism for smaller, newer companies to raise finance through the Exchange and have their shares traded. Investors could have confidence that, although such companies are inherently more risky than large listed companies, the issue and trading of shares was properly regulated.

During the 1980s the USM was very successful, but by the early 1990s, as a result of regulatory changes and commercial circumstances, it had run out of steam. The London Stock Exchange decided to close the USM and replace it with a new market – the Alternative Investment Market (AIM).

In June 1995 the LSE launched the Alternative Investment Market (AIM) to provide primary and secondary market facilities for companies either too small or too new to apply for a full listing. AIM is properly regulated by the LSE but its conditions are less demanding than those of the Official List and AIM companies tend to be very small.

The main requirements for a company to be admitted to AIM are as follows:

- There are no size or trading requirements as there are for listed securities.
- There is no requirement for any given percentage of the shares to be in the hands of the public.
- AIM companies must comply with some but not all of the Continuing Obligations of listed companies.
- Each company must appoint and retain a nominated advisor and a nominated broker:
  - The *nominated adviser* advises and guides the directors on their responsibilities and obligations with respect to AIM rules and will handle the admission of the company to AIM.
  - The *nominated broker* promotes the trading in the shares and maintains the company's page on the SEATS plus system.

There are now over 600 companies on AIM with a total market capitalisation of around £5 billion (compare with the listed market capitalisation of around £1,500 billion).

3.15 Flotation methods

The main methods of coming to the market are:

i) Offer for sale
Shares are offered to the public. Listing particulars are prepared and either the full listing particulars or an offer notice with an application form or a small box advertisement will be published in at least one national newspaper, usually the Financial Times. The offer is open to all investors.

If the offer is oversubscribed shares are allocated by prorating applications, using a ballot or by some other method.

To protect against undersubscription the offer will be underwritten.

ii) Placing
Shares are placed with the clients of the issuing house handling the issue. The general public cannot participate. A small box advert is placed in the FT (or other national newspaper).

Placings are an easier, quicker and cheaper way of issuing shares compared with an offer for sale and are now the most common issue method. Offers for sale are now relatively rare.

iii) Intermediaries offer

Other brokers may participate in a placing by applying for shares on behalf of their clients

iv) Introduction

Existing shares are admitted to listing. No new shares are issued. A small box advert is placed in the FT (or other national newspaper).

3.16 The Offer Price

Much thought and discussion will go into the price at which the shares are to issued. The company and its advisors will take into account the trading performance of the company and the forecast for the next year, the state of the industry in which the company operates, the state of the economy, the trading performance and share price of similar companies, market and investor sentiment. The final offer price results from a mix of quantitative analysis and subjective judgement.

Ideally the company will want the issue to be priced such that it is oversubscribed but not heavily so. If the price is regarded as cheap then there will be heavy stagging and thus heavy oversubscription. A stag is an investor who applies for a new issue with a view to selling the shares at a handsome profit when the shares start trading in the secondary market.

On the other hand if the price is regarded as too expensive then the issue will be undersubscribed. The company will protect against this outcome by having the issue underwritten. Undersubscription is bad for public relations and will depress the share price as many of the underwriters will be looking to sell their shares at a suitable opportunity.

A recent development in issue techniques is *book building*. This a method whereby the issuing house approaches a number of buyers and asks them how many shares they are willing to buy and what price they are willing to pay. At the end the issuing house fixes a price at which the whole issue should be taken up. The principal advantages are that it saves on underwriting costs and that the shares are likely to end with long term holders rather than stags. Unfortunately it is not a practical method to issue to private investors.

Chapter 4

TRADING SHARES –
THE SECONDARY
MARKET

4.1 Introduction

Once shares have been issued, they will be traded between investors and we now move on to examine that trading – the secondary market.

The chapter explains:

- the difference between quote driven and order driven markets
- the role of market makers
- the three trading systems used by the London Stock Exchange – SETS, SEAQ and SETS plus
- how virt-x offers an alternative market for trading listed shares
- the Ofex facility for unlisted shares.

4.2 On exchange or OTC

Securities may be traded using the facilities and under the rules of an organised stock exchange. Such trading is described as on–exchange. Alternatively, securities may be traded between investors directly outside of a formal exchange framework. Such dealing is off–exchange or over–the–counter. (OTC).

4.3 Types of market

4.3.1 QUOTE DRIVEN OR ORDER DRIVEN
An examination of stock exchanges around the world shows that there are two types of operation within secondary markets. These two types of market are described as

- Order–driven markets.
- Quote–driven markets.

4.3.2 OPEN – OUTCRY MARKET OR TELEPHONE/ COMPUTER

A market where trading is done face–to–face on the trading floor of the Exchange is called an *open–outcry market*; New York and Tokyo have trading floors. Not all markets have a trading floor. For example the London Stock Exchange gave up its trading floor in 1986 and trading is now carried out by telephone or by computer.

4.4 Order–driven market

In an *order–driven* market a buyer and a seller of shares each has a broker acting on their behalf as an agent.

The role of the broker acting for the buyer is to find a matching counterparty, ie, find a matching seller, and vice versa for the broker acting for the seller. The broker acting for the seller sells his client's shares to the broker who is buying on behalf of the buying client.

This matching might either take place on the floor of an exchange, or by means of a computerised system, or by both floor and computer trading.

The brokers make a profit by charging their clients commission for arranging the deal.

In October 1997 the London Stock Exchange introduced order driven trading the Stock Exchange Electronic Trading Service

(SETS) for FTSE 100 and certain other stocks. The New York Stock Exchange and the Tokyo Stock Exchange are predominantly order–driven markets.

Note: the FTSE 100 stocks are the largest 100 companies on the London Stock Exchange, measured by market capitalisation.

4.5 Quote–driven market

In *quote–driven* markets there are firms called *market makers*.

The role of the market maker is to buy and sell securities under all market conditions.

They always quote a price for buying and a price for selling and they make their profits through such dealing.

Buyers and sellers still have brokers acting on their behalf but instead of trying to find a matching counterparty, the broker arranges the transaction with a market maker. The broker makes a profit by charging a commission to their client.

The London Stock Exchange (below the FTSE–100) and NASDAQ, an American screen–based market, are quote–driven markets.

4.6 Member firms of the London Stock Exchange

There are around 300 member firms of the LSE. All firms are described by the rules as broker/dealers. This name embraces the so–called dual capacity of firms to

- Act as a broker or agent, and
- To deal on their own account, ie, act as principal.

A firm may choose to register with the LSE as a market maker. There are around 30 UK equity market makers. The market making firms will also be agency brokers.

4.7 Market Makers

The UK equity market in shares other than the FTSE 100 and those other shares dealt through SETS, is a quote driven market which relies on market makers to quote prices and to buy and sell shares.

Any member firm of the LSE may apply to register as a market maker but given the capital needed to support a market making operation only the larger firms are so registered.

A firm registers as a market maker on a stock by stock basis and it is a commercial decision for a firm to decide in which shares it wishes to make a market.

For larger companies there will be several market makers all competing with each other for business. Lower down the rankings there will be fewer and fewer market makers until at the small end of the market a company may have two, or one, or even no market makers.

The principal obligation of a market maker is to quote on the Stock Exchange Automated Quotation System (SEAQ) a two–way price for each security in which they are registered, that price being the price at which they will deal – a so–called *firm price*.

4.8 Two Way Price

Market makers quote a *two–way price*. For example, a share might be priced:

$$240p - 244p$$

The lower price (240p) is called the *bid price* and is the price at which the market maker will buy the share from investors. The higher price (244p) is called the *offer price* (or *ask price*) and is the price at which the market maker will sell the shares to the investor.

The difference between the bid and offer prices is called the *spread* and this is the basis of the market maker's profits.

4.9 Dealing Systems

There are three dealing systems on the London Stock Exchange:

* *SETS* for FTSE 100 and some other shares
* *SEAQ* for other listed shares with 2 or more market makers
* *SEATS* plus for listed shares with less than 2 market makers and all AIM shares.

4.10 The Stock Exchange Electronic Trading Service – SETS

SETS started operation on Monday 20 October 1997.

The main features of SETS are:

* The order book is used for FTSE100 shares, FTSE100 reserve shares (these are shares on a reserve list for the FTSE 100 – the next ones to be promoted), past constituents of the FTSE 100 and reserve list and other

UK constituents of the FTSE Eurotop 300. At present there are around 200 companies traded on SETS.

- Each security has its own page.
- On that page brokers input orders to buy and sell.
- If an incoming order matches against an order already on the order book in terms of price the orders are executed against each other automatically.
- The opening hours of SETS are as follows:

0750 – 0800	*Opening*	Addition and deletion of limit orders allowed. No automated execution occurs.
0800 – 1630	*Normal market*	An uncrossing algorithm (auction) is run at 0800, after which the trading opening price is set and automated execution begins. All types of orders can be entered and deleted from the time when automated execution begins.
1630 –1700	*Closing*	At 1630 a closing auction is held which determines the official closing price. Thereafter existing orders may be deleted but no new orders may be entered. No automated execution occurs.
		Limit orders that have not reached their expiry date stay on the book. Orders that have reached their expiry date and time are deleted.

- Only member firms can enter or delete orders.
- All market participants can view the entire order book.
- Orders are executed in the following priority:
  - best price first
  - oldest first, when there is more than one order at the best price.
- Best price for an order book security is:
  - the highest bid price on the order book for that security
  - the lowest offer price on the order book for that security.
- The tick size will be either 0.25p, 0.5p or lp depending on the price of the security. Tick size is the minimum price movement.
- There are five order types:

Limit order
Price limit is set. Order executes immediately if possible. Execution may be partial. Any unexecuted portion is placed on the order book.

At best order
No price limit. Order executes immediately as far down the order book as necessary. Any unexecuted portion is rejected (occurs if order is bigger than the order book).

Execute and eliminate order
Price limit is set. Order executes immediately if possible. Execution may be partial. Any unexecuted portion is rejected.

Fill or kill order

All or nothing. Order executes in full immediately or it is rejected.

Market order

Market orders are unpriced orders that may be entered during the opening and closing auctions. They are designed to improve liquidity.

- Only limit orders may sit on the order book, other orders are either immediately executed or rejected, in full or in part.
- Orders cannot be amended, they can only be deleted and replaced. A new order is given a new time stamp and moves to the back of the queue of orders at the same price.
- When a limit order sitting on the order book is partially executed, the remaining part of the order keeps the same time priority as the original order.
- All trades that result from orders executed on the order book generate automatic trade reports for regulatory purposes. Trade reports for other trades must be submitted manually. (See Section 4.16 below for details of trade reporting.
- All trades, regardless of size, are published immediately after being reported to the Exchange.
- The page also displays a *yellow strip* which identifies at any moment the best bid and best offer prices. The prices shown in the yellow strip is called the *touch price*. The touch price is the basis of best execution for dealing in UK equities. *Best execution* means the broker must act for the

client at the best price available in the market. It is a regulatory requirement that firms deal for their clients on a best execution basis.

- All orders on the book are anonymous.
- Following execution, details of the trade are sent to the London Clearing House which acts as the Central Counterparty for all SETS trades. This preserves the anonymity of the counterparties from each other and from the market as a whole. The Central Counterparty function is explained in the next chapter.
- If an order entered in error is executed, a reverse transaction may be performed by agreement with the counterparty or counterparties. The contra trade must be dealt away from the order book.
- Trades dealt through the order book are for standard settlement, ie, T+3. (See Chapter 5 below for details of settlement)
- Trades are transmitted to settlement systems via member firms' own settlement links.
- Trading may be interrupted in the following circumstances:
- *Listing is suspended*
    - Order book for that security is closed
    - All orders are deleted
    - No trading within or outside of the order book
- *A trading halt is declared because of a disorderly market*
    - Order book for that security remain open for the entry and deletion of orders
    - No trading within or outside of the order book

- *Suspension of automated execution for 5 minutes*
  - ○ Occurs if best bid/offer price is more than 5% different from the last automatically executed trade
  - ○ Order book for that security remains open for the entry and deletion of orders
  - ○ No execution through the order book
  - ○ Trading permitted outside the order book.

4.11 Example of a limit order

The following example illustrates how a limit order would execute through SETS.

The trading screen for a hypothetical company, ABC, shows the following:

Orders to buy (bids)		Orders to sell (offers)	
Shares	**Price p**	**Shares**	**Price p**
10,000	610	6,000	620
5,000	600	9,000	630
8,000	590	15,000	640

These orders are described as *limit orders* because the broker has specified the price (limit) at which they are prepared to deal. None of these orders can execute against each other because the highest price any buyer is prepared to pay (610p) is below the lowest price any seller is prepared to accept (620p).

Limit orders are placed with a time limit which can be up to 90 days.

Now let us assume that Firm XYZ enters a limit order to sell 12,000 shares at 610p. 10,000 shares will execute immediately against the best buy order. The remaining 2,000 shares cannot execute and will be added to the selling side of the order book. The price of 610p is now the lowest sell price and thus the order will go to the top of the sell side. After the execution the order book will be:

Orders to buy		Orders to sell	
Shares	**Price p**	**Shares**	**Price p**
5,000	600	2,000	610
8,000	590	6,000	620
		9,000	630
		15,000	640

4.12 Executing an order in a SETS security

Although SETS is the main market for FTSE 100 shares, trades can be executed outside of SETS.

SETS securities can be executed in the following ways:

- Through SETS
- Outside the order book over the telephone – the firm may be acting as agent or principal.
- Outside the order book with a Retail Service Provider – these are firms which provide online trading services for private client brokers.
- Outside the order book as a Worked Principal Agreement – a protected way of trading as principal for very large trades.

4.13 The Stock Exchange Automated Quotation System – SEAQ

SEAQ has been operating since Big Bang – 26 October 1986.

SEAQ is a computerised price dissemination service which operates as follows:

- Each listed share not traded on SETS and for which there are two or more registered market makers has a separate page on SEAQ. Shares with less than two market makers do not appear on SEAQ; neither do AIM shares

- On that page each market maker will display their two way price. This price is described as a *firm price*, meaning that the market maker is obliged to deal at the price shown on the screen and cannot change their mind when a broker calls them. Of course, market makers change their screen prices as the day's events unfold but, at any time, whatever the price on the screen the market maker must deal at it.

- Market makers must display firm prices from 8.00am to 4.30pm. This is called the *Mandatory Quote Period*.

- Prices are *firm* to other member firms – this means that market makers are only obliged to deal with other members firms of the LSE, hence the need for the investor, be they institutional or private, to use a broker.

- Prices are only *firm* for deals up an amount called the *Normal Market Size* (NMS). The market makers quotes are not firm for deals in excess of NMS – in such cases they are said to be indicative.

- NMS is calculated for each stock and is based on a percentage of the stock's average daily customer turnover in the preceding year. The NMS is intended to represent a normal institutional trade.

- There are 15 levels of NMS ranging from 100 shares to 200,000 shares.

- For example, if a share has an NMS of 100,000 a market maker might display his price as:

235 – 239   1L x 1L

- ○   235 – 239 is the firm two way price.
- ○   1L is the size up to which the price is firm (L=100,000 shares). The size is given both for the bid and the offer. The 'x' has no meaning.

- Market makers can quote prices for more than NMS if they wish.
- As on SETS, the page also displays a *yellow strip* (known as the *touch strip*) which identifies at any moment the best bid and best offer prices (from the investors point of view) quoted by the market makers. This best price is called the *touch price* or the touch. The yellow strip is the basis of best execution for dealing in UK equities.

4.14 How a deal is executed using SEAQ

SEAQ is a price dissemination system. It gives the broker and, through him, the client the real time market maker quotes.

Having made the investment decision the trade will be executed by the broker, acting on behalf of the client, with the market maker using the telephone.

The broker must execute the order with one of the market makers currently quoting the touch – this is best execution. The market making firm can be the same firm as the broker provided the deal is done at the touch.

Most deals are executed through the market makers but there are two other ways in which the trade can be done:

- by the broking firm, not being a registered market maker, dealing as principal with the investor – this is called principal trading, and
- by the broking firm matching up the deal with another client who wants to undertake the opposite trade, ie, matching a buyer with a seller, – this is called an agency cross.

Best execution for principal trades and agency crosses means giving the investor a price which is better than the touch price quoted by the market makers.

4.15 The Stock Exchange Alternative Trading Service – SEATS plus

Listed stocks with less than two market makers and all AIM stocks are traded through another stock exchange system called *SEATS plus*. SEATS was started in 1993 to improve the trading of less liquid securities.

Like SEAQ, each share on SEATS plus has an individual page and the service shows:

- Current member firm quotes.
- A market maker quote, if any.
- Company information.
- Past trading activity.
- Name of the corporate broker.

4.16 Reporting of transactions

An investment exchange can only regulate trading activity if the exchange authorities are aware of what the activity is. Up–to–date information on the current trading activity is necessary so that the exchange can be aware of unusual activity and, perhaps, improper trading.

Trades executed through SETS are automatically reported by the system.

Other trades executed between 8.00am and 4.30pm must be reported by the market maker within 3 minutes.

Trades executed outside the Mandatory Quote Period have different reporting requirements.

4.17 Publication of prices and transparency

A market is said to be *transparent* if all participants can see what securities are being bought and sold, in what quantities and at what price. To be truly effective the trade details should be published as soon as they have been reported into the exchange. Any delay means that investors are not aware of the current trading.

After a trade has been reported into the LSE details of the price and size are published electronically by the LSE:

Trades in SETS securities are published immediately.

For other shares the rules are:

- Trades up to 6 x NMS are published immediately.
- Trades over 6 x NMS are delayed 60 minutes before publication.
- Trades over 75 x NMS– called block trades – can be delayed 5 days.

The reason for the delay is to give a market maker who has taken on a large position time to unwind that position.

4.18 Other UK markets

The London Stock Exchange is the principal market for dealing in UK equities. There are, however, two other markets for UK equities:

- virt-x – for dealing in UK listed equities, *and*
- OFEX – for dealing in unlisted equities.

4.19 virt-x

virt-x was created in June 2001 through a merger between Trade-point and the Swiss Exchange.

Tradepoint started operations in September 1995 and offered an order driven alternative to dealing on the LSE. It offered dealing facilities for listed, but not AIM, securities.

virt-x is owned jointly by the TP Consortium (made up of the leading international brokerage and financial services firms) and the Swiss Exchange together with some outside shareholders. It is a fully fledged Recognised Investment Exchange regulated by the Financial Services Authority.

virt-x currently provides trading in Swiss and UK blue chip equities and a wide range of other continental European equities.

Settlement is T+3 and may be made through a choice of systems that includes CREST and Euroclear.

4.20 OFEX

OFEX is an unregulated dealing facility in which J P Jenkins Limited, a LSE market maker, is principal market maker. *OFEX is not a Recognised Investment Exchange.*

Shares trade on OFEX are unlisted, ie they are neither listed on the London Stock Exchange nor admitted to AIM

All trading is carried out, outside of the LSE itself, between J P Jenkins Limited and other Stock Exchange member firms acting on behalf of their clients.

OFEX vets all applicants to its facility and the documentation is reviewed by a panel made up of an accountant, a solicitor, a fund manager and a clearing bank.

Shares traded on OFEX can be very illiquid and should be regarded as high risk investments.

4.21 Other features of dealing

Having explained the dealing systems of the London Stock Exchange, this chapter concludes with some brief notes on some other features of dealing which may be encountered in various markets world–wide.

4.21.1 BULLS, BEARS AND STAGS

The stock markets have famous (or infamous!) animals prowling their environs: bulls, bears and stags.

A *bull* is an investor who believes that prices will rise, ie they are optimistic and a bull market is one where prices are steadily rising.

A *bear* on the other hand is an investor who believes that prices will fall, ie they are pessimistic, and a bear market is one where prices are steadily falling.

In the previous chapter, a *stag* was described as an investor who applies for a new issue with a view to selling the shares at a handsome profit when the shares start trading in the secondary market.

4.21.2 CIRCUIT BREAKERS

In response to the market crashes in October 1987 and October 1989, the New York Stock Exchange and subsequently some other Exchanges instituted *circuit breakers* to reduce market volatility and promote investor confidence.

In broad terms a circuit breaker operates as follows:

*   it is triggered when the stock exchange index moves by a certain percentage in the course of the trading day.
*   when triggered, trading is restricted for a limited period. This may be for five or ten minutes or it could be for longer for larger falls.

For example, if the Dow Jones index declines before 2.00pm by 1,050 points from the previous day's close then trading in all stocks is halted for 1 hour. This is simply one example of a number of circuit breakers in New York.

A circuit breaker could operate on the whole market or it could operate on a specific share if the price of that share moves by a certain percentage. For example in London if the price of a share moves by 5% from the last automatically executed trade then trading in that share is halted for 5 minutes.

4.21.3 MARGIN TRADING

It is common practice in some markets for shares to be bought on *margin*. The broker lends money to the investor to buy shares but the investor must put up a certain amount of funds (the *margin*) themselves.

If the shares start to lose value then the investor will be asked to pay more margin.

Margin trading is not particularly widespread in London.

4.21.4 ROUND LOTS AND ODD LOTS

In many markets shares are dealt in standard amounts called a *round lot* or *a board lot*. For example, in New York most shares are traded in round lots of 100 shares.

A quantity of shares which is not a multiple of a round lot is called an *odd lot*.

London does not operate with round lots.

4.21.5 PENNY SHARES

Penny shares are very low–priced shares and are often highly speculative.

In New York a share trading at less than a dollar would be regarded as a penny share; in London a penny share would be one trading at less than 10p or 20p. Penny share is frequently used as a term of disparagement, although some penny stocks have developed into investment–calibre issues.

4.21.6 PROGRAM TRADES

The term '*program trading*' covers a wide range of portfolio trading strategies involving the purchase or sale of a number of stocks (say 15 or more) simultaneously.

One example is *index arbitrage*. Index arbitrage is defined as the purchase or sale of a basket of stocks in conjunction with the sale or purchase of a derivative product, such as index futures, in order to profit from the price difference between the basket and the derivative product.

4.21.7 TICK SIZE

Tick size is the minimum movement in a share price. In New York it is 1 cent in London it is $1/4$ of a penny.

The term tick can also mean the direction in which the price of a stock moved on its last sale. An up–tick means the last trade was at a higher price than the one before it and a down–tick means the last sale price was lower than the one before it. A zero–plus tick means the transaction was at the same price as the one before.

Chapter 5

SETTLEMENT OF TRANSACTIONS

5.1 Introduction

In the previous chapter, the methods by which a trade is executed were explained. After execution the trade must be settled, ie the shares must be transferred from the seller to the buyer and payment must be made from the seller to the buyer.

This chapter covers:

- The expenses of dealing, ie commission, stamp duty and PTM levy
- The meaning of settlement
- The timetable of settlement
- A full description of the CREST system – who participates in it and how it works.

5.2 Expenses of Dealing

The usual expenses of dealing are

- Commission.
- Stamp Duty.
- PTM Levy.

5.2.1 COMMISSION

Commission is the charge made by the broker for executing a deal.

There are no rules governing commission rates – the only requirement is that they are not unreasonable. It is therefore a commercial decision for firms to set their own commission rates.

Commission rates are usually tiered, eg 1.65% on the first £5,000 and reducing thereafter with a minimum commission of, say, £25. Commission rates for institutional investors are usually much lower (as a percentage) than those for private investors.

In addition to commission a broker might make additional charges, especially for nominee services and discretionary management.

Commissions on gilts are usually lower than those on equities.

Commissions for execution only services will be lower than those for advisory services.

5.2.2 STAMP DUTY (SD)/ STAMP DUTY RESERVE TAX (SDRT)

SD/SDRT is government tax charged on the transfer of UK registered shares.

SD is charged if the transfer is effected by means of a transfer form and SDRT is charged if the transfer is effected through CREST.

The tax is at a rate of $\frac{1}{2}$% of the purchase price.

SD/SDRT is paid by the purchaser, not by the seller.

SD is rounded up to the next £5; SDRT is calculated exactly.

There is no SD/SDRT on gilts.

Some other countries, eg Eire, also levy a stamp duty or transfer tax.

5.2.3 PTM LEVY

PTM levy is a charge made to help fund the Panel on Take–overs and Mergers (PTM), the regulatory body for the conduct of take–over bids.

The levy is at a flat rate of £1 on deals over £10,000 consideration.

It applies only to sterling denominated securities but not gilts.

5.3 Settlement

5.3.1 THE MEANING OF SETTLEMENT

A securities transaction occurs either face to face in an open–out-cry market or over the telephone or through a computer system. Once the deal is agreed it must be settled. The process of settlement involves two actions:

- The transfer of ownership of the stock from seller to buyer, and
- The transfer of cash from the buyer to the seller.

Ideally, both processes happen:

- Simultaneously, this is known as Delivery versus Payment (DVP), and
- As short a time as possible after the trade.

Many markets provide central facilities to handle the process of settlement.

5.3.2 TRADE CONFIRMATION

Trade confirmation is the first stage of settlement. When a trade is made face to face or over the telephone is quite easy for mistakes to occur. In trade confirmation both parties report in the details of the trade to a central facility which then compares them. If the details agree then the trade is confirmed and settlement can proceed. If the details do not agree then the two parties will be notified and asked to correct whatever error has occurred.

If a trade is executed through a computerised order system such as SETS, confirmation occurs automatically and no separate confirmation activity is required.

5.3.3 TIMING OF SETTLEMENT

Ideally trade confirmation and settlement should occur immediately after the trade. However, in practice this is not possible.

Different markets have had different traditions and timings for settlement but the international consensus has moved towards rolling settlement.

Rolling settlement means that the trade is settled a specified number of days after the date of the trade. This is often expressed as T + *the number of days*. For example, T+3 means that the trade will be settled 3 business days after the date of the trade.

Markets which use or have used other settlement timings are changing to rolling settlement. For example, the UK and France used to have a system called account settlement, but they have now changed to rolling settlement.

At present, the standard settlement timing in the UK is T+3.

In practice, a broker can agree a different settlement timing with a market maker. For example, it is not uncommon for private client trades to be agreed at T+10. The reasons for this are explained in Section 5.7 at the end of this chapter.

5.4 CREST

5.4.1 INTRODUCTION
CREST is the settlement system in the UK. It went live in July 1996 and, following the phased transition of securities to CREST, replaced the London Stock Exchange's Talisman settlement system in April 1997.

CREST settles transactions in UK and Irish equities and corporate loan stocks either free of payment or else against sterling, euros and US dollars. As well as settling UK and Irish securities, CREST also provides settlement services for gilts, money market instruments, unit trusts, open ended investment companies and a growing range of international securities.

Investors are able to maintain security holdings in dematerialised accounts within CREST or alternatively they can maintain their holdings in certificated form. CREST does not force investors to get rid of their certificates.

Settlement occurs throughout the day, with the system offering effective delivery versus payment (DVP) so that at the point that the buyer acquires title to the securities the buyer's bank guarantees to pay the seller's bank, who in turn is obliged to pay the seller.

In July 2002, CREST and Euroclear announced their intention to merge. The combined group will offer a service that will enable its members to settle transactions in both domestic and international securities. By the end of 2005 a single system will replace the two existing systems. Until the inauguration of the single system, CREST will continue to offer settlement as detailed below.

5.4.2 CREST

CREST maintains records of its members' stock holdings and reconciles them with the records of legal title held by company registrars. It facilitates the settlement of transactions between its members by:

a)   authenticating and matching instructions from parties who wish to settle a transaction;

b)   amending records of account holdings and recording associated payment obligations;

c)   providing information for settlement banks and registrars so that legal title and payment can be moved by them outside the system.

Additionally, CREST calculates and collects Stamp Duty Reserve Tax and Stamp Duty on behalf of the Inland Revenue and Irish Revenue Commissioners.

Whilst CREST is not a regulator, under the Financial Services and Markets Act 2000, it has Recognised Clearing House status. CREST provides the London Stock Exchange, the Irish Stock Exchange, virt-x, LIFFE and the Financial Services Authority (FSA) with information relating to their members' transactions.

CREST also monitors the performance of those using the system and will enforce industry agreed standards for matching and settlement.

5.5 CREST Participants

5.5.1 OVERVIEW
Participants have a formal relationship with CREST. They include: CREST members and sponsored members (over 40,000), registrars (30 including 8 Irish registrars), receiving agents, payment banks, regulators, the Inland Revenue (and Irish Revenue Commissioners), and information providers. Participants need not themselves operate the technology which communicates with the system but can use the services of another party.

5.5.2 USERS

Users, of which there are around 275, are those organisations with the technical capacity to communicate with CREST. They may act within CREST on behalf of one or more participants, which may include themselves. Users must have signed a contract with a network provider (BT–Syntegra or S.W.I.F.T) in order to communicate with CREST and are able to provide the technical capacity to enable 'sponsored' use of the system.

5.5.3 MEMBERS

A CREST member is a participant who holds stock in accounts within the system and appears on the company registers as the legal owner of the securities. Typically, a CREST member is likely to be a broker, institutional investor, custodian, market maker, stock borrowing lending intermediary (formerly known as a money broker), or inter dealer broker. In principle anyone could be a member of CREST provided that the following requirements are met.

a)   The member must have a contract with a payment bank who in turn is under contract to make and receive payments in respect of the member's activities in CREST.

b)   The member must have the technical capacity to interface directly with CREST (ie must be a user).

c)   Each member must accept the terms and obligations of the CREST service.

5.5.4 SPONSORED MEMBERSHIP

Investors (institutions, nominee companies or individuals) may opt to become *sponsored members* of CREST. Sponsored members hold securities in accounts within the system and appear on the register as the legal owners. They have the full rights and responsibilities of membership but rely upon a sponsoring user to provide the technical capacity to interface with CREST. A sponsored member has a trilateral membership contract with CREST and the sponsor and must also have an a payment arrangement with a payment bank.

5.5.5 PAYMENT BANKS

Payment banks are those participants who are obliged to make payment in respect of securities delivered to their customers (members and sponsored members) through CREST. The movement of funds is between the payment banks' accounts with the Bank of England and occurs simultaneously with the transfer of securities in CREST. Members settle with their payment banks on a daily basis outside CREST. No money is held or is passed through CREST.

5.5.6 MEMBER ACCOUNTS

Members and sponsored members hold stock in accounts within CREST and appear on the registers as the legal owners. If an organisation requires several legal entities to be recognised on the register (for example, nominee companies) then several sponsored memberships will need to be established.

Within each membership or sponsored membership, a number of separate identities (designations) called member accounts can be established. Each member account appears as a designated account on the register and must be set up by the member or sponsored member before it can be used for any CREST settlement activity. The member account facility enables members or sponsored members to segregate holdings of different kinds (for example individual client holdings or funds).

The contents of each member account are mirrored on the appropriate company register. Whenever there is a transfer of stock to or from a member's account for UK securities there is a change of legal title at the point that settlement occurs. CREST also generates an electronic message called a register update request (RUR) for the registrar so that it can amend its record to reflect what has happened in CREST. For non-UK securities settling through CREST (eg, Irish securities) legal title to the securities does not pass from seller to buyer until the register has been amended. The register is updated within two hours of the RUR being made available by CREST.

In addition to the register entries relating to dematerialised holdings in CREST accounts, there are also be entries relating to investors holding stock in certificated form. Members and sponsored members can deposit and withdraw stock in paper form to and from their member accounts and this facility enables those investors with certificates to settle their transactions through CREST.

5.5.7 BANKING ARRANGEMENTS

CREST does not maintain bank accounts for members. Instead, each member and sponsored member must have arrangements with a bank which will guarantee the members' payment obligations.

However, CREST does maintain a *Cash Memorandum Account* (CMA) for each member. A CMA shows the balance of cash payments and receipts arising during the day. At the end of the day the banks settle with each other and their clients outside CREST.

5.5.8 SETTLEMENT OF A TRADE

In the example below investor A is a member of CREST and owns 10,000 shares in ICI plc. The shares are recorded in the ICI register as belonging to A and are recorded in A's stock account within CREST. A has a bank account which guarantees his obligations within CREST.

Investor A owns
10,000 ICI shares

CREST

Stock Account for Investor A
10,000 ICI shares

**Cash Memorandum
Account for Investor A**

**Investor A
Bank Account**

ICI Share Register
Investor A: 10,000

- Investor A sells the shares for £30,000 to investor B who is also a member of CREST. The actions which will take place are described in the following diagram.

SETTLEMENT OF TRANSACTIONS

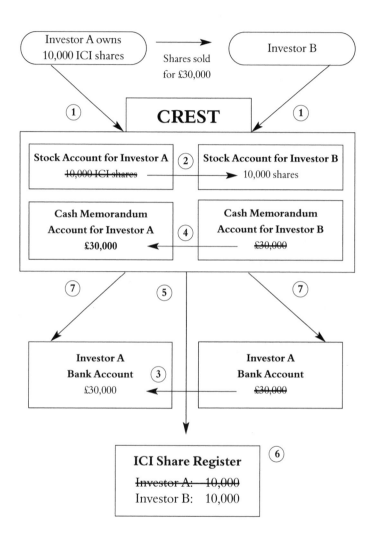

1. When the trade has been executed both members input the details of the trade into CREST. If the details match CREST creates a matched transaction.
    On settlement day CREST checks that A has sufficient stock in its stock account, that B has enough credit in its CMA and that B's payment bank has sufficient funds with the Bank of England.
2. The stock is moved from A's account to B's account and for UK securities, legal title passes between seller and buyer at this point.
3. Payment is made at the end of the day.
4. The guaranteed payment obligations are recorded in the CMAs.
5. CREST creates a register update request.
6. The registrar amends the register within two hours.
7. Instructions are sent to the banks to make payment.

5.6 Central Counterparty

On 29 February 2001 a central counterparty service went live within CREST settlement. In general terms a central counterparty (CCP) is an organisation which interposes itself between the two principals to a trade and stands as the counterparty to each thereby guaranteeing that the trade will settle for each party. The CCP stands as the buyer for the selling party and the seller for the buying party. The CCP for Crest is the London Clearing House.

The CCP service is used for all trades executed through SETS.

With the introduction of the CCP service, both the buyer and the seller will have the CCP as their counterparty. This happens at the time of execution. The buyer and seller enter orders into SETS. When their orders execute, SETS reports to each member that the trade has executed and shows the LCH as the counterparty.

The CCP services offers two advantages:

(i)   Post-Trade Anonymity
      Having a CCP ensures that the parties to a trade remain anonymous and this should improve the transparency of the price formation process.

(ii) Reducing Risk
      Having a CCP service will centralise and reduce counterparty risk, ie the risk that a counterparty will default on a trade.

5.7 International links

CREST was a founder member of the *European Central Securities Depository Association* (ECSDA). ECSDA was formed in 1997 in order to provide a forum for national Central Securities Depositories to exchange views and take forward projects of mutual interest. Its work programme has focused on the delivery of secure and efficient DVP cross-border settlement. There are fourteen members of the ECSDA.

CREST has established links with a number of overseas Central Securities Depositories including the DTC in the USA, Clearstream in Frankfurt and SIS in Switzerland.

With the announcement of the merger of CREST and Euroclear (July 2002) the process of settling international securities and transferring securities between borders will become less cumbersome. By the end of 2005 there will be a single settlement system for domestic and international securities.

5.8 Settlement of trades where there is a share certificate

If the shareholder holds a share certificate instead of holding the shares within CREST then settlement proceeds as follows:

- The broker will send to the client a *CREST transfer form*. This is a legal form which must be signed by the registered holder of the shares authorising the company registrar to change the registration.
- The client returns the signed transfer form, together with the share certificate, to the broker.
- The broker checks that the paperwork is correct and then sends the transfer form and certificate to CREST which provides facilities for paper settlement and onward transmission of the transfer form and certificate to the registrar.

It can be seen that the sending and returning of certificates and transfer forms is very time consuming especially if mistakes arise, which they frequently do with clients sending back incorrect documents or signing transfer forms incorrectly. Completing everything in time for T+3 is almost impossible. It is usually private investors who hold certificates and it is for this reason that many private client trades take place outside SETS on a T+10 basis.

Chapter 6

SOME MAJOR OVERSEAS EXCHANGES

6.1 Introduction

The last few chapters have looked in some detail at the London Stock Exchange. This chapter gives an overview of dealing and settlement systems in some of the world's major markets:

*   USA - New York and NASDAQ
*   Japan
*   Germany
*   EURONEXT Paris

6.2 USA

The United States has the world's largest stock market. The stock exchanges are the New York Stock Exchange, the American Stock Exchange (also in New York), NASDAQ, the Philadelphia Stock Exchange, the Boston Stock Exchange, the Chicago Stock Exchange, the Cincinnati Stock Exchange and the Pacific Exchange (in San Francisco and Los Angeles).

The largest exchanges, and indeed the largest in the world, are the New York Stock Exchange and the NASDAQ-AMEX Group.

6.3 The New York Stock Exchange

The New York Stock Exchange was established in 1792 and is one of the oldest in the world.

It is an order driven, floor dealing market. Brokers, acting on behalf of investors, deal with one another matching their clients' trading instructions.

A central feature of the New York Stock Exchange is the role of the 'specialist'. A specialist is a member firm of the exchange who acts partly as a regulator and partly as a dealer.

The system works as follows:

Each stock is allocated to a specialist.

- There is only one specialist per stock and each specialist will have responsibility for around a dozen stocks.
- Each specialist works at a 'post' on the floor of the exchange.
- All trading in the stock of a company must take place at the specialist's post and the specialist is responsible for ensuring an orderly market.
- The specialist can deal on his own account or on behalf of others
- The functions of the specialist can be described as follows:
  - Maintaining current bid and ask prices for their assigned stocks.
  - Acting as agents, executing orders entrusted to them by a trading floor broker, such as a limit order.
  - Buying or selling for their own accounts, against the trend of the market, when there is a temporary shortage of either buyers or sellers. This promotes stability and liquidity in the market.
  - Acting as catalysts, bringing buyers and sellers together, so that offers to buy can be matched with offers to sell.

Most shares are traded in round lots of 100 shares.

Orders are transmitted to the trading floor using telephone and computer systems.

6.4 NASDAQ-AMEX

NASDAQ-AMEX Group came into being in 1998 through the merger of NASDAQ and the American Stock Exchange, AMEX. Both exchanges, however, operate independently.

NASDAQ is a screen based, quote driven market. It has now overtaken London and Tokyo to become the second largest stock exchange in the world after New York, measured by market capitalisation.

It is owned and operated by the *National Association of Securities Dealers* (NASD) which is an American securities industry self regulatory organisation that operates subject to the oversight of the Securities and Exchange Commission.

Companies listed on NASDAQ are often smaller, newer companies, especially in the higher technology sector. Some have grown into mighty giants like Microsoft and Intel.

NASDAQ screens are available world-wide.

Each share quoted on NASDAQ has a screen page on which market makers post bid and offer prices. A company must have at least 2 market makers. The average is 11 market makers with the most active stocks having 40 or more.

A broker handling a clients order will execute the order with a market maker showing the best price. This may be over the phone or through an automated execution system.

The American Stock Exchange, AMEX, is the second largest floor exchange in the USA. It operates on a specialist/broker system similar to New York.

6.5 Settlement in the USA

Settlement timing in the USA is T + 3.

US shares are registered shares. Most shares are held in the central securities depository called the Depository Trust Company (DTC) which operates a book entry transfer system.

Clearing takes place through the *National Securities Clearing Corporation* (NSCC).

There is now a link between CREST and DTC allowing for trades in US securities to be settled through CREST.

6.6 Japan

6.6.1 INTRODUCTION
The Tokyo Stock Exchange is pre-dominantly an order driven market.

Shares listed on the Tokyo Stock Exchange are allocated either to the First Section or the Second Section. The First Section contains the larger companies (approx 1,300) and the Second Section the smaller companies (approx 500).

Dealing takes place through an electronic order book called *CORES*.

Settlement is T + 3 by book entry transfer.

All transactions executed on the Tokyo Stock Exchange (TSE) are cleared and settled through the Japan Securities Clearing Corporation (JSCC), a wholly owned subsidiary company of the Tokyo Stock Exchange.

Shares may be held by investors personally, or through nominees or through a central depository, the Japan Securities Depository Centre (JASDEC).

6.7 Germany

6.7.1 INTRODUCTION
The Deutsche Börse is the third largest exchange in Europe after the London Stock Exchange and EURONEXT.

Trading takes place through a computerised order book system called XETRA.

The normal settlement in German equities is a T+2 rolling settlement.

Clearing, settlement and custody takes place through *Clearstream Banking Frankfurt.*

German shares are bearer shares, which are immobilised in Clearstream. However, registered shares are now being used.

6.8 EURONEXT Paris

In 2000 the Paris, Brussels and Amsterdam exchanges merged to create EURONEXT making it the second largest exchange in Europe after London.

The EURONEXT trading system is a computerised order book called NSC.

Settlement is T+3 and the central counterparty and clearing house is for EURONEXT is CLEARNET SA. The central securities depository for EURONEXT Paris is Euroclear (formerly SICOVAM).

Listed companies will remain listed on their national exchanges but all shares will be traded on the single integrated trading platform and the listing requirements will be harmonised. Trading will be regulated with a single rulebook and the take-over rules will continue to be imposed domestically.

Although the three exchanges have merged, full migration to single systems will take some time and, to a certain extent, they retain their individual identities; for example they retain their own listing rules and the national indices continue, being representative of the different economies. The three markets are now called EURONEXT Paris, EURONEXT Amsterdam and EURONEXT Brussels.

EURONEXT Paris has three regulated markets:

- The Premier Marche, the main market
- The Second Marche, the second market or junior market
- The Nouveau March for innovative high growth stocks.

Chapter 7

STOCK EXCHANGE INDICES

7.1 Introduction

Shares rise and fall and so do stock markets. These market movements are measured by stock exchange indices.

This chapter explains:

- The principles behind the calculation of indices
- The FTSE family of UK indices
- Some overseas indices.

7.2 Uses of indices

An index is a number that gives the value of something relative to a base value. Every stock exchange prepares one or more indices which are calculated from the prices of a certain number of shares and they describe how the price of securities in general have moved over time.

Indices are very useful tools because:

- they provide a measurement of the performance of the market
- they provide a benchmark against which to judge the performance of individual shares and of portfolios
- derivatives such as futures and options can be based on them.

7.3 Calculation of indices

In constructing an index a base date is selected and a base value for the index, say 100 or 1,000, is ascribed to that date. The value of the index at any later time is calculated by adjusting the base value of the index for the movement in the value of the items comprising the index.

Indices can be calculated in two ways:

i)   some indices are calculated simply as an average of the
       shares prices of the companies comprising the index – an
       unweighted index.

ii)   it is more common for an index to be calculated based on
       the market capitalisation of the companies. In this case a
       price movement in a big company's share will have a
       larger effect on the index than the same price movement
       in a smaller company's share – a weighted index.

Stock market indices can be calculated as:

*   Unweighted arithmetic
*   Weighted arithmetic

7.4 Unweighted arithmetic index

Consider the following 4 shares and their prices

Share	No of shares	Price at 1.1.02 £	Market cap at 1.1.02 £	Price at 31.12.02 £	Market cap at 31.12.02 £
A	1,000	2.40	2,400	4.00	4,000
B	4,000	3.00	12,000	3.10	12,400
C	2,000	8.90	17,800	9.90	19,800
D	5,000	3.70	18,500	3.50	17,500
			__50,700__		__53,700__

AN INTRODUCTION TO EQUITY MARKETS

An index of these four shares will be constructed with a base value of 1,000 at 1 January 2002.

An unweighted arithmetic index is at 31 December 2002 is calculated as:

$$\text{Index} = \frac{\text{Sum of current prices}}{\text{Sum of base prices}} \times \text{Base Index value}$$

$$\text{Index} = \frac{4.00 + 3.10 + 9.90 + 3.50}{2.40 + 3.00 + 8.90 + 3.70} \times 1,000$$

Index = 1,138.9

7.5 Weighted arithmetic index

A weighted arithmetic index could be calculated as:

$$\text{Index} = \frac{\text{Sum of current market capitalisations}}{\text{Sum of base market capitalisations}} \times \text{Base Index value}$$

$$\text{Index} = \frac{53,700}{50,700} \times 1,000$$

Index = 1,059.2

7.6 FTSE Indices

Probably the best known index in the UK is the FTSE 100 index. This is just one of a family of indices produced by FTSE International. FTSE International is a joint venture company owned by the Financial Times and the London Stock Exchange. It is responsible for devising and calculating stock exchange indices in a number of different countries.

The UK series of indices comprise:

FTSE All Share
Approximately 800 listed companies comprising approx 98–99% of the total market capitalisation of the London Stock Exchange

FTSE 100
Largest 100 UK listed companies. The FTSE 100 comprises approx 75% of the total market capitalisation of the London Stock Exchange. At the time of writing the largest company is BP with a market capitalisation of about £120bn. Companies at the bottom end of the FTSE 100 have a market capitalisation of about £2bn.

FTSE 250
Next 250 companies below the FTSE 100

FTSE 350
Largest 350 companies (100 + 250)

FTSE Small Cap
Remainder of the All Share

FTSE FLEDGLING
About 1,000 companies below the All – Share

FTSE All Small
FTSE Small Cap plus the FTSE Fledgling

FTSE AIM
Index for AIM shares

The UK indices are calculated on a weighted arithmetic basis.

The constituents of the indices are regularly reviewed. For example, the largest 100 companies will obviously change as share prices change. FTSE International has very precise ground rules and the constituents of the FTSE 100, FTSE 250 and FTSE 350 are formally reviewed every 3 months with promotions and demotions in and out of the indices.

The following diagram shows the relationship between the indices.

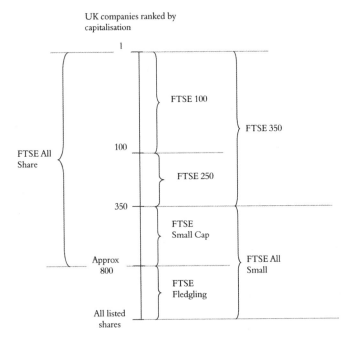

In addition to the FTSE Indices there is also the FT30 Index. This is now an unrepresentative index of 30 shares and it is calculated on an unweighted geometric basis. It is however the oldest UK index, going back to 1935.

7.7 FTSE Euro Indices

FTSE International publishes a number of pan European indices, the principal one's being:

- *FTSE Eurotop 300* – the 300 largest capitalised companies in Europe
- *FTSE Eurobloc 100* – the 100 largest capitalised companies from the countries participating in the Euro (the common European currency)
- *FTSE Eurotop 100* – 100 leading companies in Europe. The index is intended to be representative of trends on the major European Stock Exchanges.

7.8 Overseas indices

Well–known overseas indices are:

Dow Jones	New York and NASDAQ
Standard and Poors 500	New York
Nikkei 225,	Tokyo
Hang Seng	Hong Kong
CAC40	EURONEXT Paris
DAX	Germany
OMX	Sweden
Straits Times	Singapore

7.9 Sectors

One would expect that an oil exploration company has a very different type of business from a clothes retailer. Consequently, the London Stock Exchange is, for statistical purposes, divided into industry sectors and statistical data is published for each sector.

There are 10 economic groups divided into 35 sectors which in turn are divided into about 100 sub–sectors.

The economic groups are:

- Resources
- Basic Industries
- General Industrials
- Cyclical Consumer Goods
- Non–cyclical Consumer Goods
- Cyclical Services
- Non–cyclical Services
- Utilities
- Information Technology
- Financials

Chapter 8

DIVIDENDS, BONUS ISSUES AND RIGHTS ISSUES

8.1 Introduction

Chapter 8 considers corporate actions – things such as dividends, bonus issues and rights issues.

In particular, the chapter examines:

- Cash dividends versus scrip dividends
- The dividend time table and the significance of ex–dividend
- Scrip issues and their effect on the share price
- Pre–emption and rights issues
- Sale of rights nil paid and splitting rights

8.2 Corporate Actions

Corporate action is a term which describes any event that results in a change of a company's capital. It also incorporates all benefit distribution situations.

A corporate action may be defined as any action by an issuer of investments or by another party in relation to the issuer affecting an investors entitlement to investments or benefits relating to those investments. This includes, but is not restricted to, take–overs, rights issues, stock conversions, scrip dividends and redemptions.

8.3 Dividends

A dividend is a payment to shareholders out of the profits of the company.

In Chapter 2 an explanation was given of realised and unrealised profits. Check that you understand what these terms mean before moving on.

8.3.1 INTERIM AND FINAL DIVIDENDS.

It was also explained in chapter 2 that the frequency with which companies pay dividends varies: some companies pay one dividend a year, some pay two dividends a year and some pay four dividends. If more than one dividend is paid then the earlier dividend(s) are called *interim dividends* and the last dividend is called a *final dividend*. Most companies pay one interim dividend and one final dividend.

The interim dividend is paid after the results for the first 6 months of company's financial year have been announced. The final dividend is paid after the Annual General Meeting has approved the accounts and the dividend for the full financial year.

A typical timetable for a company which has a financial year ended 31 December 2002 might be:

Interim dividend
The results for the 6 months
to 30 June 2002 are announced   2 August 2002

The interim dividend for the
year 31 December 2002 is paid   15 October 2002

Final dividend
The results for the year
31 December 2002 are announced   21 February 2003

The AGM is held   9 May 2003

The final dividend for the year
31 December 2002 is paid   27 May 2003

8.3.2 SCRIP DIVIDENDS
A dividend is usually paid to a shareholder as a cash payment.
Occasionally companies pay a dividend in the form of new shares
in the company. Such a dividend is called a *scrip dividend* or a *stock
dividend.*

For example, a company has a share price of 200p and pays a dividend of 8p per share. If the company was to offer a scrip dividend to
its shareholders it would offer shareholders 1 new share for every 25
shares that they hold. The proportion of 1 for 25 is calculated as:

$$\frac{\text{Price per share}}{\text{Dividend per share}} = \frac{200}{8} = 25$$

Thus if Mr X holds 10,000 shares he may take a cash dividend of
£800 (10,000 x 0.08) or he may take 400 new shares (10,000 ÷ 25).
The advantage for the shareholder is that he acquires new shares

without incurring dealing costs. The advantage for the company is one of cash flow; the cash which would have been used to pay the dividend is retained within the company.

8.3.3 EX DIV AND RECORD DATES

Because shares are continually changing hands the payments of a dividend to the shareholders requires careful planning to ensure that dividends are paid only to those entitled to receive them.

Registered securities

In the case of registered shares the company will make the dividend payment to the registered holders. Because the share register is inevitably behind the actual trading of the shares it is important that there is a well established timetable in place for the payment of dividends so that investors, both buyers and sellers, know exactly what their entitlements are and nothing is left to chance.

There are three days of importance in the payment of dividends for registered securities:

- The dividend payment day
- Record day, also known as books closed day
- Ex–dividend day.

The *dividend payment day* is the day on which the shareholder will receive the dividend either by cheque or bank transfer.

Record day is the day on which the company closes its share register for the purposes of the payment of dividends, hence the alternative name: books closed day. In other words, the company will pay the dividend to those persons recorded as shareholders on the register of shareholders on record day. The period between record day and payment day be will as long as is necessary to deal with the administration; it is usually between three and ten weeks.

For purchases and sales close to the record day there will be uncertainty as to whether the transfer will or will not be recorded on the share register in time for record day. To eliminate that uncertainty, the stock exchange will declare the shares *ex–dividend* some days before the record day. On that day the share trades without the right to the next dividend payment; they are said to be *ex–dividend*. Prior to the ex date the shares are said to be trading *cum–dividend*.

In theory, on the ex–date the share price should fall by the amount of the dividend.

In the UK the London Stock Exchange marks a UK equity share *ex dividend* (XD) on a Wednesday with the record day being the Friday of the same week. This timing is designed to fit in with T+3 settlement. The XD date must be at least 3 clear business days after the dividend announcement.

Payment of the dividend

The dividend may be paid by the company to the shareholder in one of three ways:

(i)   By cheque to the shareholder.
(ii) Directly into the shareholder's bank or building society account through the Bankers' Automated Clearing System (BACS). To enable the company to make a payment in

this way the shareholder must give the company permission to do so and also give the company details of their bank or building society account. This is done by means of a form called a dividend mandate form.

(iii) Via CREST into the bank account used for CREST purposes. For a dividend to made this way the company must have opted to distribute dividends this way and the shareholder must have notified the registrar that they wish to receive dividends in this way.

By having the dividend paid into a bank or building society account by methods (ii) or (iii) above the shareholder:

- Avoids the risk of loss or delay in the post
- Avoids the inconvenience of having to take or send the dividend to the bank or building society and
- Avoids the risk of mislaying or accidentally destroying the dividend cheque.

Dividend voucher

For each dividend payment the shareholder will receive a dividend voucher. This is an important document which shows:

- The number of shares on which the dividend is being paid
- The cash amount of the dividend and
- The tax credit.

It must be retained by shareholders for the purposes of completing their self assessment tax returns.

Where the dividend is paid directly into a bank account the voucher is sent to the registered shareholder. Where the dividend is paid by cheque the voucher is attached to the cheque.

Bearer securities

In the case of bearer securities the company does not maintain any record of the holders of the securities. In practice bonds are more likely to be in bearer form than are shares.

To obtain payment of the interest the bondholder must make a claim. In order to do so, each certificate will have coupons attached either to the certificate or on a separate sheet. The coupons will be numbered sequentially. The company will then announce that, say, coupon number 5 is due for payment on a specified date. To obtain payment of the interest coupon number 5 will be detached (clipped) and submitted by the bondholder or their custodian to the bank authorised by the company to make interest payments.

Where bearer bonds are held in a Central Securities Depository, the depository will operate a record date to establish which bondholders are entitled to receive the interest payment.

8.4 Scrip Issues

A scrip issue is an issue of new shares to existing shareholders in proportion to their existing shareholdings. The shareholder does not pay for these new shares and they are said to issued fully paid up.

The company does not raise any additional capital from a scrip issue.

The reason for making a scrip issue is usually to reduce the share price.

Example

Take for example, a company with a share price of 720p which makes a 1 for 3 scrip issue. This means that the company will be issuing 1 new share for every 3 shares currently in issue.

This will have a diluting effect on the share price which can be calculated as follows:

Before the issue	3 shares	@ 720	2,160
Scrip	1 share		
After the issue	4 shares		2,160

The theoretical price after the issue is:

$$\frac{2,160}{4} = 540 \text{ per share}$$

The share price before the issue (720p) is called the *cum–scrip* price and the price after the issue (540p) is called the *ex–scrip* price.

Why should the company want to reduce the share price? The company and its shareholders, of course, want the share price to increase but a stage is reached when the share price seems to investors to become a bit too high and the share becomes more difficult to buy and sell. It is described as becoming less liquid. In order to improve the liquidity of the shares the company makes a scrip issue. There are then more shares available but at a lower price.

A scrip issue is also called a *bonus issue* or a *capitalisation issue*.

8.5 Stock Split

A share split is another way of reducing the share price. Very simply the company divides each share into a number of shares each with a smaller nominal value.

For example, if a company has a share with a nominal value of 25p and a market price of 800p per share it could reduce the share price by having a share split whereby each share is split into 5 shares each with a nominal value of 5p. There are 5 times as many shares in issue and the price of each share should fall to 160p (= 800/5).

8.6 Rights Issue

8.6.1 PRE–EMPTION

A rights issue arises from a shareholder's *pre–emption right (*also called *pre–emptive right)*. This is the right of the shareholder whereby a company making a new issue of shares must offer the shares to the existing shareholders in proportion to their existing holdings. The rationale behind a rights issue is to prevent a shareholder's interest in the company becoming diluted.

Unlike a scrip issue, a rights issue is intended to raise funds for the company and it will increase the net assets of the company. It will also have an effect on the share price.

Example

Consider a company with a share price of 300p per share; this is the cum–rights price. It wishes to raise capital from the shareholders and makes a rights issue on a 1 for 4 basis at 250p per share. Shareholders are not obliged to subscribe for a rights issue and therefore in order to give them an incentive to do so the rights issue is made at a discount to the current market price, in this case at 250p per share.

The issue of new shares at a discount will have a diluting effect on the share price which can be calculated as follows:

Before the issue	4 shares	@ 300	1,200
Rights issue	1 share	@ 250	250
After the issue	5 shares		1,450

The theoretical ex–rights price after the issue is

$$\frac{1,450}{5} = 290\text{p per share}$$

This means that each existing share will fall from 300p to 290p but the new rights share which has a subscription price of 250p will also have a market price of 290p per share.

8.6.2 SALE OF RIGHTS NIL PAID

A shareholder is only offered the new shares; they are not obliged to take them up. The shareholder can sell the entitlement to subscribe to some one else. This is referred to as the *sale of rights nil paid* and the theoretical *nil paid price* is defined as

Nil paid price = Ex–rights price – subscription price

$$290 - 250 = 40p \text{ per share.}$$

8.6.3 SPLITTING RIGHTS

Some investors choose to sell part of their rights entitlement nil paid in order to raise sufficient funds in order to take up the balance of their entitlement. Selling only part of a rights entitlement is called splitting the rights

The formula for the number of rights to sell nil paid in order to have enough cash to take up the balance is:

Number of shares to sell nil paid =

Rights entitlement x $\dfrac{\text{Subscription price}}{\text{Ex rights price}}$

Example (continued)

Carrying on from the example above consider an investor who holds 10,000 shares. They will be offered 2,500 rights shares. The number to sell nil paid can be calculated as follows:

Number of shares to sell nil paid $= 2,500 \times \dfrac{250}{290}$

Number of shares to sell nil paid $= 2,156$

That leaves 344 rights to be taken up.

The cash then works out as follows:

Sale of 2,156 rights nil paid at 40p $= £862.40$

Take up 344 rights at 250p $= £860.00$

There is £2.40 left over which is not quite enough to take up a rights share (£2.50).

8.7 Share buy backs

The last few years have seen considerable activity in share buy–backs. These have come about because some companies have accumulated large reserves of cash for which they have little immediate use and a share buy–back is one way of returning that cash to shareholders. Another way of returning cash to shareholders is by way of a special dividend. This, however, does not reduce the share capital of the company.

The assets of a company should be invested in the company's business thus earning profits. The rate of return on those assets, as measured by ratios such as the return on capital employed (see next chapter for details of the calculation), should be higher than current levels of interest rates. If the return was lower than interest rates then the company should close down its business and put the cash on deposit! Investors invest equity in a company for that company to earn high returns from the risks of operating a business.

If the company has a substantial cash balance, that cash is earning a lower return than if it was invested in business assets. This has a diluting effect on the earnings per share (again the detailed calculation is explained in the next chapter). If the company has little use for the cash then it should be returned to the shareholders who can then decide what to do with it, for example put it on deposit or invest in other companies.

One way of returning that cash is to have a share buy back. The company must obtain permission from the shareholders by a vote in general meeting. The company will then be authorised to buy back a specific number of shares. Having obtained authorisation the company will then purchase shares in the open market. The shares thus purchased are cancelled by the company and the cash balance decreases as does the share capital. This should have the effect of improving the earnings per share and the share price.

It should be stressed that in a buy back the company makes its purchases in the open market; no shareholder is compelled to sell back to the company.

A share buy back may also enhance the company's net asset value if the shares can be purchased for less than net asset value.

Chapter 9

COMPANY ACCOUNTS AND WHAT SHARES ARE WORTH

9.1 Introduction

We have seen what shares are and how they are issued and traded. We now move on to a consideration of the factors that analysts take into account in recommending which shares to buy and which shares to sell.

This chapter covers:

- Fundamental and technical analysis
- The format of company accounts
- Ratios used in analysis

9.2 Types of investment analysis

There are two types of investment analysis, known as *fundamental analysis* and *technical analysis.*

Fundamental analysis is a detailed analysis of the company under review and the industry in which it operates with the objective of deciding whether the shares are over–valued or under–valued. The valuation is based on the profits and the forecast profits of the company. In this context the profits are referred to as *earnings.*

One very important source of data about a company is its annual financial accounts, which are also described as the financial statements. The investment analyst will carry out a detailed examination the accounts and extract much useful information. It is not the objective of this book to provide a detailed description of the construction and analysis of financial statements but an outline description is given.

Technical analysis involves analysing past share prices and making investment decisions on the basis of trends in those prices.

9.3 Financial statements

Fundamental analysis starts with a detailed analysis of the financial statements of the company. The financial statements, or accounts, of a company comprise three main statements, which are supported by pages of detailed notes:

* the balance sheet
* the profit and loss account, and
* the cash flow statement

9.4 Balance sheet

The balance sheet shows, at a point in time, the financial state of affairs of the company. It is structured as an equation and in outline form it appears as follows:

Balance sheet at 31 March 2002

	£m
Assets	200
Less: Liabilities	(50)
Net assets	£150
Financed by:	
Shareholders funds	£150

Assets represent resources owned by the company, such as buildings, plant and equipment and goods for resale, which are used in its business.

Liabilities represent amounts owed by the company to suppliers of goods, to bankers and to bondholders.

Net assets is the difference between assets and liabilities.

The *shareholders funds* shows how the shareholders have funded the company through subscribing for capital and through the retention of profits.

The equation effect of the balance sheet is that:

$$\text{Net assets} = \text{Shareholders Funds}$$

The assets, liabilities and shareholders funds are further classified as follows:

Balance sheet at 31 March 2002

	£m	£m
Fixed assets		130
Current assets	70	
Less: Current Liabilities	(15)	
Net current assets		55
Capital employed		185
Deferred liabilities		(35)
Net assets		£150
Share capital		20
Share premium account		45
Retained earnings		95
Shareholders funds		£150

Again, Net assets = Shareholders funds

The various terms used in the balance sheet are described as follows:

Fixed assets are assets acquired for long term use within the company and intended to be used for a number of years rather than sold in the normal course of business; examples are buildings and plant and equipment.

Current assets are assets acquired for conversion into cash in the normal course of business; examples are stocks or inventories, accounts receivable (debtors) and bank balances.

Current liabilities are obligations that are payable within 12 months of the balance sheet date; examples are bank overdrafts, short term loans and accounts payable (creditors).

Net current assets means current assets less current liabilities. This is also called the working capital of the company.

Capital employed is defined as the total of fixed assets plus current assets less current liabilities. If you apply the equation approach to the balance sheet you will see that the term also means the shareholders funds plus deferred liabilities. Thus capital employed also means the total of capital provided by shareholders and from borrowing.

Deferred liabilities are obligations that are repayable after more than one year. The main category will be the longer term borrowings of the company, for example the bonds issued by the company.

Share capital is the nominal value of the shares that have been issued.

Share premium account represents the excess of the issue price of shares over the nominal value. USA accounts use the term 'paid in surplus' for the share premium.

Retained earnings are the accumulated retained profits, or earnings, of the company since incorporation.

The share premium account and the retained earnings are called the reserves of the company.

9.5 Profit and loss account

The *profit and loss account* shows how the profit of the company have arisen over a period of time, usually a year, leading up to the balance sheet date. Under US reporting the profit and loss account is called the *income statement*.

In outline it will appear as follows:

Profit and loss account for the year ended 31 March 2002

	£m
Sales (or revenue)	X
Less: Expenses	(X)
Profit before taxation	X
Less: Taxation on profits	(X)
Profit after taxation	X
Less: Preference dividend	(X)
Earnings	X
Less Ordinary dividend	(X)
Retained Earnings	£X

9.6 Cash flow statement

The cash flow statement shows the major cash flow movements in the year under the following headings

- cash flows from trading
- purchasing and selling fixed assets
- issuing and redeeming shares and bonds
- the payment and receipt of interest and dividends
- the payment of tax
- the payment of dividends.

9.7 Regulatory requirements for company accounts

There are three sources of regulation for company accounts:

i) The Companies Acts

The Companies Act 1985 sets out rules for the formats to be adopted and the disclosure of information in the accounts.

ii) Financial Reporting Standards (FRS)

In the preparation of accounts there are many areas where judgement is used and there are alternative ways of valuing assets, or calculating income and expenditure. These alternatives are referred to as accounting policies. Acceptable accounting policies are laid down in FRSs and their predecessors, Statements of Standard Accounting Practice (SSAPs). FRSs are published by the

Accounting Standards Board, part of the Financial Reporting Council on which sit the Accountancy profession, the London Stock Exchange and the government.

iii) Listing Requirements
As part of the continuing obligations listed companies must disclose further information in addition to that required by the Companies Acts and FRSs

The financial statements are prepared by the company for the shareholders and it is the right of the shareholder to receive a copy of the accounts in advance of the annual general meeting.

The production of the accounts is the responsibility of the directors. The directors are required by the companies acts to prepare financial statements for each financial year and to present them annually to the company's members in Annual General Meeting. The financial statements must give a true and fair view of the company's results and its financial position.

In order that the shareholder can have confidence in the accounts they will be audited by an independent firm of accountants. The role of the auditors is to give an opinion on whether the accounts have been prepared in accordance with generally accepted accounting principles (GAAP) and whether they give a true and fair view (UK terminology) or a fair representation (USA terminology) of the company's results and its financial position. The auditor will verify the existence and valuation of important assets of the company and carry out tests on the internal controls of the company to ensure that transactions are properly recorded.

To the uninitiated reader the financial statements, often produced as a glossy publication, with the auditor's report, may appear to be the definitive statement of the company's profit and of its financial position. This is far from being the case. As mentioned above, in the preparation of accounts there are many areas where judgement is used and there are alternative ways of valuing assets, or calculating income and expenditure. Although there are FRSs to promulgate acceptable accounting practices, there is still much flexibility in the presentation of the figures. One of the roles of the analyst is to identify the accounting policies followed by the company and to identify if there have been any changes in policy from previous years which will affect the comparison of this year's results with those of previous years. In comparing one company with another it is important to take account of different policies being followed by different companies.

9.8 Approach to fundamental analysis

One of the key activities of fundamental analysis is the analysis of financial statements. Much of this analysis is carried out by calculating various ratios derived from the accounting and other data, such as the share price, and then interpreting those ratios.

The four areas of ratio analysis covered in this chapter are:

- Investors ratios
    Earnings Per Share (EPS)
    Price Earnings Ratio (PER)
    Dividend Yield
    Dividend cover or payout ratio

- Profitability ratios
    Profit Margin
    Return on Capital Employed

- Gearing ratio
    Debt Equity ratio

- Cash Flow and Liquidity
    Current ratio

We will examine these ratios by considering a hypothetical company, ABC Ltd which has the following Balance Sheet and Profit and Loss Account for the year ended 31 December 2002.

Profit and Loss Account for the year ended 31 December 2002

		£m	£m
Sales			71.1
Cost of sales			<u>44.1</u>
Gross profit			27.0
Other overheads			<u>12.3</u>
Operating profit			14.7
Other income			3.0
Interest payable			<u>(6.0)</u>
Profit before tax			11.7
Taxation for the year			<u>4.1</u>
Profit after tax			7.6
Dividends payable	Preference	1.0	
	Ordinary	<u>4.0</u>	
			<u>5.0</u>
Retained profits			<u>£2.6</u>

Balance Sheet as at 31 December 2002

	£m	£m
Fixed assets		140
Current assets	155	
Current liabilities	115	
Net current assets		40
Total assets less current liabilities		180
Deferred liabilities – 10% loan stock		60
Net assets		120
Ordinary share capital 120m shares of 25p		30
Preference share capital 10m shares of £1		10
Share premium account		10
Revaluation reserve		15
Retained earnings		55
Shareholders funds		120

The revaluation reserves represents the unrealised profit on the revaluation of land and buildings.

The ordinary share price is 110p and the preference share price is 120p.

9.9 Investors ratios

Investors tend to look at the income currently being earned on shares to assess the potential for growth. Different criteria can be used and a full analysis of a company involves consideration of many aspects of a company's performance and expected performance in the context of the economy.

However, two common figures which are considered by investors are the price/earnings ratio (PER) and the dividend yield.

9.10 Earning Per Share (EPS)

Before looking at the price earnings ratio we must examine the earnings per share (EPS) which shows the amount of profit earned by the company for each ordinary share. The standard definition is:

$$\frac{\text{Profit after tax, extraordinary items, minority interests and preference shares}}{\text{Number of ordinary shares in issue and ranking for dividend}}$$

In the example above the EPS is:

$$\frac{\text{Profit after tax (£7.6m) } \textit{less } \text{preference dividend (£1.0m)}}{\text{120m ordinary shares}}$$

$$= \frac{£6.6m}{120m}$$

$$= 5.5p$$

EPS is the profit available to the ordinary shareholders after the deduction of all costs, taxes and preference dividends and represents the maximum amount which could be paid out as a dividend out of this year's profits.

Investors expect the EPS to increase each year because it is an increasing EPS that enables companies to pay increasing dividends and which contributes to growth in the share price. EPS growth gives investors the income growth and capital growth that they are seeking.

9.11 Price Earnings Ratio (PER)

The price earnings ratio is defined as:

$$\frac{\text{Market price per share}}{\text{Earnings per share}}$$

The PER for ABC is:

$$\frac{110p}{5.5p} = 20$$

The PE (also known as the multiple) can be regarded as the number of years' worth of profit an investor is prepared to pay in order to buy a share in the company.

A high PE ratio means that there is demand for the shares; usually because investors are expecting growth. However, it could mean that the shares are overpriced. The analyst and investor must judge whether a high PE ratio is justified. A share with a high PE ratio usually has a low dividend yield and vice versa.

A low PE ratio may indicate that the company has limited growth prospects or that the shares are underpriced.

At the time of writing (June 2002) the average PE ratio on the FTSE All Share index is 21. Sectors with a high PE ratio include Telecoms with a PE of 80 and Media and Photography, PE 65. Are they high growth sectors or are they overpriced? That is for you to decide.

Sectors with limited growth prospects include Water Companies with a PE of 13, Construction and Building Materials, PE11, and Engineering and Machinery, PE15.

In assessing a share and the prospects for the company, an investor looks at past performance, the dividend yield and the p/e ratio, as well as forecasts for the economy and the industry. Share prices reflect investors' expectations. When the company announces its profits which turn out to be as the market expected, then the share price does not move. If the profits are lower than expected, even though they may be higher than last years' profits, the share price falls because they are lower than the expectation.

9.12 Using the Price Earnings Ratio to value a share

The PE ratio is defined as

$$\frac{\text{Market price per share}}{\text{Earnings per share}}$$

Re-arranging the formula we have: Market price = PE x eps

In order to determine a fair price for the shares the analyst must

* calculate the expected earnings and eps for the current accounting period, and
* decide on the PE ratio appropriate to the company.

The calculation of the expected earnings per share will mean an analysis of the most recent accounts together with projections based on company announcements and other data which the analyst can obtain, for example from economic and industry reports.

In determining an appropriate PE ratio the analyst must decide whether the current market PE is a fair one for the company or whether the company is being over rated or under rated by the market.

9.13 Dividend Yield

The expression yield is used extensively in the analysis of investments. In general, a yield relates a measurement of the return from an investment to its current market price, and is expressed as a percentage. The different types of yield simply use different measurements of the return. Thus the dividend yield is the relationship between the dividend per share and the share price.

The dividend yield is defined as:

$$\frac{\text{Dividend per share}}{\text{Current market price per share}} = \text{x } 100\%$$

For ABC we can calculate the dividend yield for both the ordinary shares and the preference shares.

Dividend yield for the ordinary shares

The dividend per share is:

$$\frac{\text{Ordinary dividend}}{\text{Number of shares}} = \frac{\pounds 4.0\text{m}}{120\text{m}}$$

$$= \underline{3.3\text{p}}$$

The net dividend yield is:

$$\frac{\text{Dividend per share}}{\text{Current market price per share}} \quad \text{x } 100\%$$

$$= \frac{3.3p}{110p} \times 100\%$$

$$= \underline{3.0\%}$$

Dividends are declared and paid net of a 10% tax credit and the dividend yield could be expressed as the gross yield.

The gross dividend yield is defined as:

$$\frac{\text{Grossed up dividend per share}}{\text{Current market price per share}} \quad = 100\%$$

$$\text{Gross dividend yield} \quad = \frac{3.3 \times {}^{100}\!/_{90}}{110} \times 100\% = 3.33\%$$

The net dividend yield on the FTSE All Share index is 2.9% at the time of writing.

The dividend yield on ordinary shares is usually lower than the rates of interest available on bank deposits and bonds. The reason for this is that shares offer the prospect of capital growth, which is not available with deposits and if available on bonds, will only be very limited. In return for the prospect of capital growth, the shareholder is prepared to receive lower income.

In reviewing any investment ratio the investor must consider all possible factors. A low dividend yield might mean that the company is expected to have growth prospects or it could mean that the shares are simply overpriced. Conversely, a share might have a high dividend yield because it is a company with only limited growth prospects or the company is experiencing problems and the share price is low to reflect this aspect.

Dividend yield on preference shares
The net dividend yield is:

$$\frac{\text{Dividend per share}}{\text{Current market price per share}} \times 100\%$$

$$= \frac{100p \times 10\%}{120}$$

$$= 8.3\%$$

The dividend yield on preference shares is usually higher than that on bank deposits and bonds because is a higher risk investment than either of them and because it pays just a fixed dividend it offers no income nor capital growth.

9.14 Dividend Cover

Dividend cover is defined as:

$$\frac{\text{Earnings per share}}{\text{Dividend per share}}$$

It shows both the ability of the company to pay an increased dividend and the safety of the dividend if the company has a downturn in profits.

For ABC the dividend cover is:

$$\frac{5.5p}{3.3p}$$

$$= \underline{1.67}$$

This is around the market average.

Another way of viewing the same data is by calculating the payout ratio which is:

$$\frac{\text{Dividend per share}}{\text{Earnings per share}} \times 100\%$$

$$\frac{3.3p}{5.5p} \times 100\%$$

$$= \underline{60\%}$$

Thus ABC pays out 60% of its earnings as dividend.

9.15 Analysis of financial statements

A full analysis of financial statements of a company will examine three main areas:

- Profitability
- Gearing, or leverage
- Cash flow.

9.16 Profitability

Profitability is examined from two viewpoints:

- Profit margin
- Return on capital employed.

9.17 Profit margin

Profit margin is defined as:

$$\frac{\text{Profit}}{\text{Sales}} \times 100\%$$

This ratio gives an indication of the ability of the company to sell its products at a profit. Profit margins vary considerably from one industry to another; for example, luxury goods tend to have high profit margins whereas food retailing has low profit margins.

If profit margins have changed or if a company's margins are different from the industry averages the analyst will try to find out why. For example a fall in profit margin could be caused by an increase in costs which the company has not been able to pass on in higher prices, or it could be caused by a change in the mix of products which the company is selling, or it could be caused by the company having to decrease prices because of increased competition. The analyst may be able to find some of the answers in the accounts but he will also probably need to use other sources of information, such as statements issued by the company, economic and industry reports and from visiting the company and talking to the management.

Two profit margins can be calculated from ABC's accounts:

$$\text{Gross profit margin} = \frac{\text{Gross profit}}{\text{Sales}} \times 100\% = \frac{£27.0m}{£71.1m} \times 100\% = 38\%$$

$$\text{Operating profit margin} = \frac{\text{Operating profit}}{\text{Sales}} \times 100\% = \frac{£14.7m}{£71.1m} \times 100\% = 20.7\%$$

9.18 Return on capital employed

Return on capital employed is defined as:

$$\frac{\text{Profit before interest and tax payable}}{\text{Capital Employed}} \times 100\%$$

Capital employed is the shareholders funds plus the loans. Alternatively it can be looked at as the 'Total assets less current liabilities'.

Return on capital employed shows the ability of the company to generate profits from the assets available to it. As with the profit margin the analyst will want to know the reason behind any unusual figures.

For ABC the return on capital employed is:

$$\frac{£14.7m + £3.0m}{£180m} \times 100\%$$

$$= \underline{9.8\%}$$

Other, similar, measurements which might be used are return on assets and return on equity.

9.19 Gearing

Gearing means the proportion of the assets that have been funded from borrowing and the proportion funded by the shareholders. A common measurement is the debt/equity ratio defined as

$$\frac{\text{Borrowings including preference shares}}{\text{Ordinary shareholders funds}} \times 100\%$$

The debt equity ratio for ABC is

$$\frac{\text{£60m + £10m (preference shares)}}{\text{£120m (shareholders funds) – £10m (preference shares)}} \times 100\%$$

$$= 64.5\%$$

Because preference shares pay a fixed dividend and are repaid at only the nominal value they are effective debt(although legally they are shares) and are treated as such in this calculation.

The ordinary shareholders funds are the shareholders funds excluding the preference shares.

From the point of view of the shareholders gearing is important. A reasonable level of gearing can be beneficial to shareholders because a small increase in the assets of the company will be magnified into a much higher increase in the net assets available to the shareholders.

Consider for example a company with a balance sheet as follows which experiences a 100% increase in the assets of the company:

	£	£
Assets	1,000	2,000
Less Loans	400	400
Net assets available for shareholders	600	1,600

The net assets have increased by 167%. However, high gearing means high risk because a fall in assets will also be magnified.

The American expression for *gearing* is *leverage*.

9.20 The current ratio

The current ratio is defined as:

$$\frac{\text{Current assets}}{\text{Current liabilities}}$$

$$\frac{£155m}{£115m}$$

$$= \underline{1.35}$$

The current ratio shows the ability of the company to pay its short term liabilities out of its liquid assets, ie, those assets which are turned into cash in the ordinary course of business.

9.21 Technical Analysis

Technical analysis is not concerned with the fundamentals of the company but instead relies on past price movements. There are two strategies adopted by technical analysts:

- charts
- mechanical trading rules.

9.22 Charts

A chartist believes that there are trends in share prices and by plotting a graph, or chart, showing a share price over a period of time trends can be identified and from those trends decisions made as to when to buy and sell.

9.23 Mechanical trading rules

The investor buys and sells according to some arbitrary rules; for example they might decide to sell after a share has fallen 5% from a peak and to buy when a share has risen 5% from a trough.

9.24 Fundamental Analysis or Technical Analysis?

Most analysis carried out is fundamental analysis. The rationale for using fundamental analysis is that a company's share price depends on its commercial performance and if accurate forecasts of earnings can be made then a fair valuation of the share price is possible. Over priced and under valued shares are then identified.

The technical analyst tends to believe that history repeats itself and that a study of past share prices can identify repeating patterns and trends. A knowledge of those patterns and trends can then be used to inform investment decisions. There is evidence that technical analysis can work although many investors and commentators remain sceptical.

However, technical analysis is gaining wider acceptance and many analysis departments will undertake both forms of analysis and base their recommendations on the combined evidence.

9.25 Economic data and their effect on equities

Companies operate in the economy and their trading performance is heavily influenced by the prevailing economic conditions.

The final section of this chapter considers briefly the effect of some economic data on companies and their shares.

The areas to be covered are:

- Gross Domestic Product (GDP)
- Money Supply
- Inflation
- Interest rates
- Government Borrowing
- Retail Sales
- The Exchange Rate.

9.26 Gross Domestic Product (GDP)

GDP is calculated by adding together the total value of all goods and services produced by a country within a certain time, usually one year. This gives a measure of the overall economic activity within a country. The USA has the largest GDP of any country.

GDP can be regarded as a measurement of the general wealth of a country.

If GDP increases from quarter to quarter the economy is said to be expanding and if GDP decreases from quarter to quarter the economy is said to be contracting. A decrease in GDP for two consecutive quarters is often used as a definition of recession.

The annual percentage increase in GDP is a commonly used measurement of economic growth.

Companies operate in the economy and are therefore dependant on the overall economic performance of the country for their own trading performance. Thus if the economy is growing then companies' profits should also grow which should be reflected in the company's investment performance.

Economic growth is therefore extremely important. Investors will want the economy to be growing at a reasonable rate. If growth is too fast, however, it will tend to lead to inflation which in turn will lead to higher interest rates which will reduce company profits.

A lack of economic growth, or recession, is detrimental to companies' profitability and growth.

9.27 Money Supply

The amount of money in circulation is called the money supply. Different measurements of money supply are used which are given an M designation: M0, M2, and M4 are currently in use in the UK.

Growth in the money supply will be significant to companies because if growth is too fast it will lead to increased inflation which in turn will have an adverse effect on company profits.

9.28 Inflation

Inflation is the phenomenon of prices increasing from year to year. In the late twentieth and early twenty first centuries, we are used to the idea of inflation and a certain amount of low inflation is regarded as normal. However, if inflation increases beyond its normal range then it leads to uncertainty for companies and private individuals. Companies try to increase their prices but find their costs increasing; individuals find shop prices increasing which may not be matched by increases in income and thus real buying power decreases. If inflation starts to get too high then it can lead to a fall in confidence in the economic system and may give rise to economic and political instability.

High inflation is bad news for an economy and therefore for companies and their investors.

Inflation is measured by measuring prices. A very common measure is The Retail Prices Index which measures retail prices and expresses the result as a index figure. The inflation rate is then the annual percentage increase in the index.

9.29 Interest Rates

High interest rates increase companies borrowing costs and therefore reduce profits. Therefore an increase in interest rates usually provokes a fall in share prices.

9.30 Government Borrowing

The governments raise income through taxes and if its expenditure is greater than the tax revenues the difference is borrowed by issuing bonds. Controlled government borrowing is a normal and welcome aspect of the markets; welcome because government bonds are a very useful, relatively secure investment for investors.

However, if government borrowing starts to increase then investors will become concerned. An increase in borrowing means that there will be less for investors to invest in companies; interest rates will have to increase to attract additional funds and the increased government spending will have an inflationary effect.

Therefore equity investors like to see government borrowing under control.

9.31 Retail Sales

Statistics from retail stores and government statistics on retail sales give an immediate measure of the economic activities in high streets and shopping malls. Healthy sales are important but excessive growth may be worrying because it is inflationary.

9.32 The Exchange Rate

Day to day movements in the exchange rate of sterling against other currencies are normal and expected but if the exchange rate becomes higher or lower than its normal range then it will have detrimental effects.

If the exchange rate becomes too high then it will adversely affect exporting companies because their goods will become more expensive to foreign buyers. This will lead to reducing sales or to reductions in price to keep the sales but either way it will reduce profits. On the other hand imports become cheaper, which may have a detrimental effect on UK manufacturers who find themselves being undercut by cheaper imports.

Conversely a weak exchange rate will lead to more expensive imports, but cheaper exports.

9.33 Balance of Payments

The balance of payments is a record of a country's transactions with the rest of the world including trade in manufactured goods and raw materials and services, and capital investment.

A healthy balance of payments is needed for a healthy economy.

Chapter 10

TAKE–OVERS AND DEMUTUALISATIONS

10.1 Introduction

A takeover occurs when one company acquires over 50% of the share capital of another company. Takeovers are part of an activity referred to as mergers and acquisitions (M&A). The terms take–over and merger are often used interchangeably but a take–over is the purchase of a controlling interest in another company whereas the term 'merger' is used more to describe the fusion of two companies. Mergers and acquisitions are seen as promoting the benefits of efficiency by, for example, allowing for economies of scope and scale and replacing ineffective management and methods.

Take–overs are happening all the time but it is only the large ones which reach the front pages of the newspapers. Many take–overs are of unlisted companies which are sold by the founding shareholders to a larger company, the founders thus realising their investment. However, this chapter is concerned with take–overs involving listed companies.

Takeovers involving small companies are usually of interest only to those immediately involved: shareholders, employees, creditors and customers. Where large national companies are involved the impact of the takeover will be spread wider and there will concerns about the national and public interest. Consequently there is considerable regulation surrounding takeovers.

This chapter covers:

• A description of a takeover offer and the reaction to it.
• The role of the Office of Fair Trading and the Competition Commission.
• The Panel on Takeovers and Mergers and the Takeover Code.

The chapter finishes with some comments on a separate topic: Demutualisations.

10.2 The initial offer and the reaction

One of the principles underpinning takeover regulation is that if a company (referred to as the 'predator' in this chapter) wishes to acquire control of another company (referred to as the 'target') it must make an offer to all the shareholders of the target company to acquire all their shares. The predator is not allowed to buy shares in the market, as and when they become available, until they have acquired control. The reason for this principle is to ensure fair and equal treatment of shareholders.

The offer must initially be put to the board of the target company. If the board consider the offer to be in the best interests of the company's shareholders, employees and creditors they will recommend acceptance. The directors have a fiduciary duty to act in the best interests of the company as a whole and not to be influenced by their personal interests.

If the offer is not recommended by the board it is described as a hostile bid.

The predator will send an offer document to shareholders of the target company giving details of the offer and reasons why the shareholders should accept. In a hostile bid the predator will argue that they can run the company more efficiently and profitably than can the current directors. In a friendly or recommended offer, the predator will argue that the company will have a more secure and profitable future as part of a larger organisation and this will have the endorsement of the directors. Furthermore, the offer price will be above the current market price of the shares thus making the offer very tempting to shareholders.

In a recommended offer the directors of the target company will include their endorsement of the offer in the offer document. In a hostile bid the board of the target company will put up a defence and send a defence document to their shareholders.

Both sides must be truthful in the offer document and in the defence document. During the takeover period of a hostile bid both sides will bombard shareholders with statements and advertisements and in some takeover battles the arguments become very heated and the attacks bitter.

In putting up a defence it can be difficult for the directors of the target company to argue that new management will make a worse job of running the company. The classic defence is to show that the company is worth more than the predator is prepared to pay and that the market has hitherto undervalued the shares. They will attempt to do this by issuing profit forecasts and asset revaluations.

Another defensive strategy is to adopt some of the ideas being put forward by the predators although the shareholders' reaction may well be to ask why they had not carried out these actions in the first place. Finally, if the company is operating in an industry subject to statutory regulation they could appeal to the regulator to block the bid.

The key thing to remember is that the decision whether or not to accept the offer lies with the shareholders of the target company. The predator company will try to persuade them to accept. In a friendly bid the directors of the target will recommend that they accept and in a hostile bid the directors will recommend that they reject the offer.

In the USA companies can initiate various spoiling actions if they are subject to a bid; these actions are referred to as a poison pill. Poison pills are not possible under UK regulation

10.3 The Regulators

Takeovers are subject to two areas of regulation:

1.   The economic factors such as whether the takeover will create a monopoly situation in an industry or whether it might be against the national interest. The regulators here are the Office of Fair Trading, the Competition Commission, the Department of Trade and Industry and possibly the European Commission

2.   The conduct of the two companies, their boards of directors and their professional advisors. The regulator here is the Panel on Takeovers and Mergers.

The roles of these regulators is explained in the following sections.

10.4 The Office of Trading, the Competition Commission and the Department of Trade and Industry

Takeover activity has a profound impact on the structure and efficiency of industries and markets, which can give rise to adverse effects. A system of merger control is therefore required to ensure that a particular merger does not operate against the public interest. The Fair Trading Act 1973 provides such a system of control.

At the core of the regulation is the power of the Secretary of State for Trade and Industry to block a takeover. *The Office of Fair Trading* (OFT) and the *Competition Commission* (CC) advise the Secretary of State in coming to a decision.

THE OFFICE OF FAIR TRADING (OFT)
Set up in 1973 as a result of the Fair Trading Act 1973 and headed by the Director General of Fair Trading, the OFT is a non–ministerial department of government with a range of legal responsibilities as the principal United Kingdom fair trading authority

The main roles of the Office are to:

*   identify and put right trading practices which are against the consumer's interests;
*   regulate the provision of consumer credit;

- act directly on the activities of industry and commerce by investigating and remedying anti–competitive practices and abuses of market power, and bringing about market structures which encourage competitive behaviour.

THE COMPETITION COMMISSION (CC)

The *Competition Commission* is a public body established by the Competition Act 1998. It replaced the Monopolies and Mergers Commission (MMC) on 1 April 1999.

The Commission has two sides to its work: a reporting side which has taken on the former MMC role; and an appeals side which will hear appeals against decisions made under the prohibition provisions of the Competition Act 1998.

Its role on the reporting side is to investigate and report on matters referred to it relating to mergers, monopolies, anti–competitive practices, the regulation of utilities and the performance of public sector bodies. The CC does not initiate its own inquiries. Most referrals are made by the Director General of Fair Trading (DGFT), the Secretary of State for Trade and Industry and the regulators of utilities. In almost all cases, the CC is asked to decide whether the matter referred was against the public interest.

HOW THE OFT, THE CC AND THE DTI OPERATE

As part of his monitoring of market activity, the Director General of Fair Trading has a duty to identify mergers which have taken place or are about to happen. Once he is aware of a merger, he may carry out an informal inquiry looking into the possible effects on competition and other matters of public interest. If there appears to be reasonable grounds for believing that the merger could have a detrimental effect, the Director General can advise the Secretary of State to refer the case to the Competition Commission (although the Secretary of State is not necessarily bound to accept that advice). The Secretary of State is empowered to accept legally binding undertakings as an alternative to making a reference. He must be satisfied that any such undertakings are capable of remedying the detrimental effects identified by the Director General.

Broadly, a merger situation qualifies for investigation if it involves the acquisition of gross assets worth £70 million or more, or the creation or enhancement of a share of 25% or more in the market for goods or services of any description in the United Kingdom or a substantial part of it.

In 2001 the OFT considered 356 merger cases; of these, ten were referred to the Monopolies and Mergers Commission.

Where the Secretary of State has made a reference, the Competition Commission must consider what effects the merger might have on the public interest. It will undertake an in–depth investigation and report back to the Secretary of State within a time limit, usually around 3 to 4 months. If, as a result of its investigation, it concludes that there are no detrimental effects, the merger bid can go ahead.

If the Competition Commission makes an adverse finding (ie it concludes that something is against the public interest), it may make recommendations to remedy or prevent the adverse effects which it has identified. For example, the Competition Commission could recommend that the merger or takeover should not be allowed to take place. If the merger has already taken place, disposal could be recommended. Another option is to recommend allowing the merger to go ahead if the buyer agrees to conditions such as selling off part of its business or other assets, or as to future behaviour.

The Secretary of State is not bound to accept the Competition Commission's recommendations unless it decides to clear the merger.

If the bid goes ahead then the conduct of the bid and the parties to it are subject to the Takeover Code.

10.5 The European Commission

Large take–overs involving a European dimension are subject to European regulation.

The European Commission adopted a regulation on the control of mergers in 1989 which came into force on 21 September 1990. Under the regulation, mergers with a Community dimension are subject to the exclusive jurisdiction of the European Commission (save for limited exceptions).

Broadly this means that mergers involving parties with a combined world–wide turnover of more than 5 billion euro (around £4.2 billion) are subject to the control of the European Commission, provided that the EU turnover of each of at least two undertakings involved exceeds 250 million euro (around £210 million) and the undertakings concerned do not have at least two–thirds of their EU turnover from the same member state.

Mergers which are not caught by the EC merger regulation remain subject to national competition law.

10.6 The Panel on Takeovers and Mergers

The Panel on Takeovers and Mergers is the regulatory body which publishes and administers the City Code on Takeovers and Mergers. The commercial merits of take–overs are not the responsibility of the Panel; these are the concern of the companies and their shareholders. The wider public interest matters are considered by the Office of Fair Trading, the Competition Commission, the DTI and the European Commission as described above.

The Panel was set up in 1968 in response to mounting concern about unfair practices. The Panel remains today a non–statutory body.

The essential characteristics of the Panel system are flexibility, certainty and speed. The system aims to avoid over–rigid rules and the risk that take–overs become delayed by litigation of a tactical nature which may frustrate the ability of shareholders to decide the outcome of an offer.

The membership of the panel comprises:

Chairman

2 Deputy Chairmen

3 Independent Members

and

Appointed by the

Governor of the

Bank of England

The Chairman or other senior nominee of:

Association of British Insurers (ABI)

Association of Investment Trust Companies (AITC)

Association of Private Client Investment Managers and Stockbrokers (APCIMS)

British Bankers Association (BBA)

Confederation of British industry (CBI)

Institute of Chartered Accountants in England and Wales (ICAEW)

London Investment Banking Association (LIBA)

National Association of Pension Funds (NAPF)

The day to day work of the Panel is carried out by its Executive, headed by the Director General, usually a investment banker on secondment.

10.7 The City Code on Takeovers and Mergers

The City Code on Takeovers and Mergers (referred to here as the Code) comprises 10 general rules and around 38 detailed rules. Because the code is contained in a file with a dark blue cover it is often referred to the *Blue Book*.

The Code and the Panel operate to ensure fair and equal treatment of all shareholders and to provide an orderly framework within which take–overs are conducted.

The introduction to the code stresses that not only the letter but also the spirit of the code must be observed. The underlying purpose of the General Principles and the Rules must be achieved; if necessary the Panel will modify or relax the effect of the precise words used.

The Code does not have the force of law but those who fail to conduct themselves in accordance with it may find by way of sanction have the facilities of the securities markets withdrawn from them.

Possible penalties include;

- Private reprimand
- Public censure
- Reference to another regulatory body, such as the London Stock Exchange or the Financial Services Authority
- A direction that other remedial action be taken.
- Withdrawal of Financial Services and Markets Act authorisation from a firm that requires it

10.8 Some Takeover Code rules

10.8.1 OFFEROR AND OFFEREE

In the take–over code the predator is called the offeror and the target is called the offeree.

10.8.2 30% RULE

Rule 5 requires that if a company acquires 30% of the capital of another company it must make a bid for the whole of the capital of the other company. This is called a mandatory bid. The moral is simple: if a company does not want to make a bid for another company it does not acquire 30% of the shares. That is why you sometimes find one company holding 29.9% of the capital of another company; that is as far as they can go without having to make a full bid.

10.8.3 CONDITIONS

An offer can be subject to conditions such that if the conditions are not satisfied the offer lapses.

The offer will be subject to the 'acceptance condition' and may be subject to other conditions.

The acceptance condition (Rule 10) require that the offeror acquires at least 50% of the voting rights. If the offeror does not acquire 50% the offer will fail. Although the rule says 50% the offeror often requires a 90% acceptance. The significance of 90% is that with such a level of acceptances it can compulsorily buy out the remaining shares under the provisions of s429 Companies Act 1985.

If at any time after the first closing date, D+21 (see below), the acceptance condition is satisfied the offeror will announce that the offer is unconditional as to acceptances and the offer will remain open for 14 further days to allow time for the stragglers to accept.

10.8.4 TIMETABLE OF AN OFFER

The offer will be put initially to the board of the predator company. A public announcement will then be made through the Stock Exchange Regulatory News Service. The Code emphasises the vital importance of secrecy before an announcement.

Once the announcement has been made the offeror has 28 days to post the offer document to shareholders. Although the code allows 28 days the document is usually posted much earlier. The day that the documents are posted is called D–Day and the time table starts running from D–Day.

D+21
The first closing date

This is the earliest date on which the offer may be closed. The offer document must state the closing date which may be later than but not earlier than D+21

By 8.30am next day the offeror announces the level of acceptances.

The offeror then has four choices:

- Announce that the offer is unconditional as to acceptances (if it is) and keep it open for 14 days more; otherwise
- Improve the offer
- Extend the offer
- Withdraw the offer

D+39
Latest date for the offeree to release important information, such as profit forecasts

D+46
Latest date the offer can be improved

D+60

Final closing date – if the offer is not unconditional as to acceptances by midnight the offer lapses.

If an offer fails the offeror is prohibited from making a further offer for 12 months.

10.9 Demutualisations

This chapter finishes with a brief review of demutualisations. In the introductory chapter to this book it was explained that businesses could be structured as sole proprietorships, partnerships and companies. This book has of course been concerned with companies.

But there is also another business structure – the mutual organisation. Building societies and some life assurance companies are structured as mutual organisations.

A building society is a mutual organisation owned by its members – its savers and borrowers – and it operates for the mutual benefit of its members. There are no equity shareholders. Building societies started in the late eighteenth century and their traditional purpose was to lend money to individuals to purchase or remortgage their homes. This money used to come exclusively from individual saving members who are paid interest. These days an increasing proportion, but still a minority, of the funds are raised on the commercial money markets.

Building societies are governed by the Building Societies Acts 1986 and 1997.

The principal role of a building society is still its traditional purpose of borrowing money from retail savings and lending it on in the form of mortgage loans. However these days, as a result of the Building Societies Acts, they are allowed to undertake other business such as unsecured lending, commercial lending and estate agency.

The really big thing that they have been allow to do is to convert from a mutual society into a public limited company, thereby converting from a building society into a bank. In other words to demutualise.

Examples of societies which have demutualised are Abbey National, Halifax, Alliance and Leicester, Woolwich, Northern Rock, and Bristol and West. Some other societies have been taken over by banks instead of converting into public limited companies, for example Cheltenham and Gloucester was taken over by Lloyds TSB.

Opinion is strongly divided on the merits and demerits of demutualisation. The advantages are:

- access to the international capital markets and thus greater capital raising powers and
- being able to offer a wider range of services to customers and compete on a level playing field with the commercial banks.

The disadvantages are:

- having a greater spread between lending and borrowing rates of interest because of the need to pay dividends to shareholders and
- the loss of the mutual ethos whereby the society existed for the benefit of its members (account holders) whereas a bank owes its duties to its owners, the shareholders. The account holders with a bank are not its owners; they are customers.

Some life assurance societies are also mutual. For example, in 1997 Norwich Union converted into a public limited company.

The effect of demutualisation is that account or policy holders or policy holders receive shares in the new company worth up to several thousand pounds, depending on the circumstances, effectively for free. This has extended wider share ownership and put several of the new companies into the FTSE 100 index increasing substantially the banking and finance component of the index.

Over the coming years it is expected that several more building societies will demutualise or be taken over by banks.

*   *   *   *

GLOSSARY

Alternative Investment Market (AIM)
The second tier market of the London Stock Exchange.

Annual General Meeting (AGM)
Annual meeting of a company at which the directors formally report to the shareholders on the companies performance for the past year.

Articles of Association
One of the two documents of constitution of a company – see also memorandum of association.

Ask price
See *Offer price.*

Assets
The resources owned by a company, such as buildings, plant and equipment and goods for resale, which are used in its business.

At best order
An order which is executed at the best market price(s) at the time.

Audit
The independent verification of the financial statements of a company by an independent firm of accountants.

Balance of Payments
Measurement of imports and exports in and out of a country.

Balance sheet
A financial statement showing at a point in time the assets and liabilities of a company and how those assets have been financed by shareholders.

Bear
An investor who believes that prices will fall, ie they are pessimistic, and a bear market is one where prices are steadily falling.

Bearer share
Share where ownership is possession of the certificate. There is no register of shareholders.

Beneficial owner
The true owner of shares; the person entitled to the benefits of ownership. The beneficial owner might not be the registered owner.

Bid price
The price at which a dealer will buy securities.

Big Bang
The name given to a series of far reaching reforms of the London Stock Exchange in 1986.

Blue Book
See *City Code.*

Board lot
A standard dealing quantity of shares. Also called a round lot. Dealing is normally in multiples of the board lot. Board lots are not used in London.

Bond
A marketable debt instrument issued by a company or a government.

Bonus issue
See *Scrip issue.*

Book entry transfer
A system of transfer of ownership of shares which entails only a change in the computer record of ownership. No new certificates are issued.

Books closed day
Last date for the registration of shares or bonds for the payment of the next dividend or interest payment – also called record day.

Bull
An investor who believes that prices will rise, ie they are optimistic and a bull market is one where prices are steadily rising.

CAC 40
Index of EURONEXT Paris.

Cadbury Report
Report on corporate governance published in 1992.

Capital employed
The total of fixed assets plus current assets less current liabilities. It also means the shareholders funds plus borrowing.

Capitalisation issue
See *Scrip issue.*

Cash flow statement
Financial statement showing the major cash flows of a company for a year.

Central Counterparty
An organisation which acts as the counterparty to both parties to a trade. The London Clearing House is the Central Counter Party within CREST.

Central Securities Depository (CSD)
An organisation which holds securities in either immobilised or dematerialised form thereby enabling transactions to be processed by book entry transfer. Also provides securities administration services.

Certificate
A certificate issued by the issuer of a security stating either that a named person is the registered owner or that the bearer is the owner.

Charts, chartism
A system of analysis which believes that there are trends and patterns in share prices and by plotting a graph, or chart, showing a

share price over a period of time trends and patterns can be identified and such knowledge decisions can be made as to when to buy and sell. An example of technical analysis.

Circuit breaker
An arrangement which, at times of high price volatility, halts trading on a stock exchange for a short period.

City Code
Non statutory rules with which companies and their advisors must comply in the conduct of a take–over offer. The code is administered by the Panel on Take–over and Mergers. Also known as the Blue Book.

Clearing House
An organisation operating a clearing system. Some exchanges act as their own clearing house, some depositories act as clearing houses and some clearing houses are entities separate from exchanges or depositories.

Clearing System
System by which securities transactions are settled. It may be a department of an investment exchange or it may be a separate entity – see *Clearing house*.

CLEARNET
Clearing system used in France for corporate securities.

Clearstream Banking Frankfurt
The clearing organisation and central securities depository for German securities.

Common stock
See *Equity shares*.

Company
A business entity, ownership of which is divided into units called shares, which are owned by persons called shareholders who have limited liability. The business is managed by persons called directors who are appointed by the shareholders.

Competition Commission (CC)
Government body which undertakes a detailed investigation into take–over offers referred to it and advises the DTI as to whether the bid should be blocked or allowed to proceed.

Consumer Price Index
A measurement of retail price inflation. Also called retail prices index.

CORES
Computer dealing system of the Tokyo Stock Exchange.

Corporate action
Any action by an issuer of investments or by another party in relation to the issuer affecting an investor's entitlement to investments or benefits relating to those investments. This includes,

but is not restricted to, take–overs, rights issues, stock conversions, scrip dividends and redemptions.

Corporate investor
A company which holds shares in another company solely for its own benefit.

Counterparty
One of the parties to a transaction – either the buyer or the seller.

Coupon
The physical coupon detached from a bearer certificate in order to claim a dividend or interest payments.

CREST
The organisation in the UK that holds UK and Irish company shares in dematerialised form and clears and settles trades in UK and Irish company shares.

CREST member
A participant within CREST who holds stock in stock accounts in CREST and whose name appears on the share register. A member is their own user.

CREST sponsored member
A participant within CREST who holds stock in stock accounts in CREST and whose name appears on the share register. Unlike a member, a sponsored member is not their own user. The link to CREST is provided by another user who sponsors the sponsored member.

CREST stock account
A computer account within CREST which records the share-holdings of members and sponsored members. Shares held in stock accounts are de–materialised.

CREST user
A participant within CREST who has an electronic link to CREST.

CRESTCo
The company which owns and operates the CREST system.

Cum dividend
Trading of a share with the right to the next dividend payment.

Cum rights price
Share price before a rights issue takes place – the price with the entitlement to the rights issue.

Cum scrip price
Share price before a scrip issue takes place – the price with the entitlement to the scrip issue.

Cumulative preference share
If the company fails to pay a preference dividend the entitlement to the dividend accumulates and the arrears of preference dividend must be paid before any ordinary dividend. There is no accumulation with a non–cumulative preference share where a missed dividend is simply lost.

Current assets
Assets of a company acquired for conversion into cash in the normal course of business; examples are stocks, or inventories, accounts receivable and bank balances.

Current liabilities
Obligations of a company that are payable within 12 months of the balance sheet date; examples are bank overdrafts, short term loans and accounts payable.

Current ratio

$$\frac{\text{Current assets}}{\text{Current liabilities}}$$

Custodian
Organisation which holds clients assets in safe custody, ensures that they are not released without proper authorisation and ensures the timely and accurate collection of dividends and other benefits.

Custody
The storing and safekeeping of securities together with maintaining accurate records of ownership. The term also implies management of those securities such as the collection of dividends.

DAX
Index of the Deutsche Börse.

Debenture
Another name for a corporate bond – usually secured on assets of the company.

Debt/equity ratio
A measurement of gearing defined as

$$\frac{\text{Borrowings}}{\text{Shareholders funds}} \times 100\%$$

Deferred liabilities
Obligations that are repayable after more than one year. The main category will be the longer term borrowings of the company, or the bonds issued by the company.

Deferred share
A class of share where the holder is only entitled to a dividend if the ordinary shareholders have been paid a specified minimum dividend.

Delivery versus Payment (DVP)
Settlement where transfer of the security and payment for that security occur simultaneously.

De–materialised shares
Shares which are recorded in a central computer system and for which no certificates exist. Transfer is by book entry transfer.

Demutualisation
Process by which a mutual organisation such as a building society or insurance companies converts into a limited liability company.

Depository Trust Company (DTC)
A depository for USA company shares.

Deutsche Börse
The German Stock Exchange.

Directors
The managers of a company appointed by the shareholders.

Distributable profits
The profits available for payment to the shareholders as a dividend. Will comprise realised profits.

Dividend
A distribution of profits to the shareholders of a company.

Dividend cover

$$\frac{\text{Earnings per share}}{\text{Dividend per share}}$$

Dividend yield
The yield on a share defined as

$$\frac{\text{Dividend per share}}{\text{Current market price per share}} = x \; 100\%$$

Dow Jones index
Index of the New York Stock Exchange.

Earnings per share

$$\frac{\text{Profit after tax and preference shares}}{\text{Number of ordinary shares in issue}}$$

ECSDA

European Central Securities Depository Association (ECSDA). – formed in 1997 in order to provide a forum for national Central Securities Depositories to exchange views and take forward projects of mutual interest.

Equity shares

Shares in a company which are entitled to the balance of profits and assets after all prior charges. Also called ordinary shares or common stock.

Euroclear

Euroclear is a depository and clearing organisation for international securities and eurobonds. In 2002 Euroclear and CREST announced a merger.

EURONEXT Paris

The French Stock Exchange.

Ex rights price

Share price after a rights issue – the price without the entitlement to the rights issue.

Ex scrip price

Share price after a scrip issue – the price without the entitlement to the scrip issue.

Ex–dividend

The condition whereby a share is traded without the entitlement to the next dividend payment.

Execute and eliminate order
A limit order where any unexecuted portion is rejected rather than being added to the order book.

Executive Director
Director with an operational responsibility for managing the company's business.

Extraordinary General Meeting (EGM)
Meeting of shareholders which is called between AGMs – not a common occurrence.

Fill or kill order
An order which is either executed in full immediately or not at all. All or nothing.

Final dividend
The last dividend paid for a year.

Financial Services Authority (FSA)
The regulatory organisation in the UK for securities firms.

Fixed assets
Assets of a company acquired for long term use within the company and intended to be used for a number of years rather than sold in the normal course of business; examples are buildings, plant and equipment.

Flotation
Process by which a company's shares are admitted to listing and trading on an exchange.

FTSE 100 index
Index of the largest 100 listed companies on the London Stock Exchange.

FTSE Eurobloc 100 Index
The 100 largest capitalised companies from the countries participating in the Euro (the common European currency).

FTSE Eurotop 100 Index
100 leading companies in Europe, the index being intended to be representative of trends on the major European Stock Exchanges.

FTSE Eurotop 300 Index
The 300 largest capitalised companies in Europe.

Fundamental analysis
Detailed analysis of a company and the industry in which it operates with the objective of deciding whether the shares are over–valued or under–valued.

Gearing
In the context of financial accounts gearing is the proportion of funds from borrowing compared with the proportion from shareholders.

Greenbury Report
Report on directors remuneration and service contracts published in 1995.

Gross Domestic Product (GDP)
The total value of goods and services produced within a country over a given period of time.

Hampel Report
Report on corporate governance published in 1998.

Hang Seng index
Index of the Hong Kong Stock Exchange.

Immobilised shares
Shares certificates held by a central depository which records changes of ownership by book entry transfer.

Income statement
See *Profit and loss account.*

Incorporation
The process of creating a company in accordance with the legislation of the country concerned.

Index
A figure calculated from the share prices or the market capitalisations of a specific number of shares on a stock exchange.

Index arbitrage
The purchase or sale of a basket of different shares and the simultaneous sale or purchase of an index derivative.

Initial Public Offering (IPO)
Issue of shares by which a company first comes to the market, ie by which it is floated.

Institutional investor
An institution which is usually investing money on behalf of others.

Interim dividend
Dividend paid part way through a year in advance of the final dividend.

Introduction
Method of listing a company where no shares are issued – the existing shares are listed and trading can commence but there is no IPO.

Japan Securities Depository Centre (JASDEC)
A central depository for Japanese shares.

Joint stock company
Another name for a company.

JSCC
Japan Securities Clearing Corporation – clearing organisation in Japan.

LCH
London Clearing House.

Leverage
See *Gearing*.

Liabilities
Amounts owed by a company to suppliers of goods, to bankers and to bondholders.

Limit order
An order placed by a broker specifying a maximum purchase price or a minimum selling price.

Limited liability
A benefit of share ownership whereby the liability of a shareholder for the debts of the company is limited to the capital subscribed.

Liquidation
The formal process of closing down a company. The assets are sold, the liabilities and preference shares are repaid and any balance of assets is paid to the ordinary shareholders – also called a winding up.

Liquidity
The ease with which shares can be converted into cash, ie, the ease with which they can be sold, or cashed in, and the speed with which the proceeds are received.

Listed company

Company which has been admitted to listing on a stock exchange and whose shares can then be dealt on that exchange.

Listing Particulars

Name for a prospectus for a listed company.

Listing Rules

Rules administered by the Financial Services Authority in its role as the UK Listing Authority with which companies must comply in order to obtain and retain a listing – also called the Purple Book.

Loan stock

Another name for a corporate bond – usually unsecured.

Margin

The broker lends money to the investor to buy shares but the investor must put up a certain amount of funds (the margin) themselves. If the shares start to lose value then the investor will be asked to pay more margin.

Market capitalisation

The market capitalisation of a company means the market price per share multiplied by the number of shares in issue. The market capitalisation of a stock market is the sum of the market capitalisations of all the companies quoted on the exchange.

Market maker
A securities firm which will buy and sell shares under all market conditions.

Member
Another name of a shareholder of a company.

Memorandum of Association
One of the two documents of constitution of a company – see also *Articles of Association.*

Monopolies and Mergers Commission (MMC)
Old name for the Competition Commission.

Multiple
See *Price earnings ratio.*

NASDAQ
National Association of Securities Dealers Automated Quotation system – An American based stock market which uses computer screens and is quote driven.

National Securities Clearing Corporation(NSCC)
An organisation providing settlement and clearing facilities in the USA.

Net assets
The difference between assets and liabilities.

Net current assets
Current assets less current liabilities. This is also called the working capital of the company.

Nikkei 225 index
Index of the Tokyo Stock Exchange.

Nil paid right price
Ex–rights price less the subscription price.

Nominal value of share
The minimum price at which a share can be issued. Also called par value.

Nominated Advisor
Firm which advises and guides the directors of AIM companies on their responsibilities and obligations with respect to AIM rules and which handles the admission of the company to AIM.

Nominated Broker
Firm which promotes the trading in the shares of AIM companies and maintains the company's page on the SEATS plus system.

Nominee
A person registered as the holder of a security who is holding it on behalf of another person.

Non–cumulative preference share
If the company fails to pay a preference dividend the entitlement to the dividend is simply lost. There is no accumulation.

Non–executive Director
Director who does not have an operational responsibility within the company.

Normal Market Size – NMS
The size of trade up to which a market makers price on SEAQ is firm to other member firms.

NSC
The dealing system of EURONEXT Paris.

NSCC
National Securities Clearing Corporation – clearing organisation for US shares.

Odd lot
A quantity of shares which is not an exact multiple of a board lot. Will often be at a disadvantageous price to a board lot.

Ofex
An unregulated trading facility for trading in UK shares which are unlisted and not traded on AIM.

Offer for Sale
A method of IPO by which shares are offered to the public.

Offer price
The price at which a dealer will sell securities – also called the ask price.

Office of Fair Trading (OFT)
Government body which advises the DTI whether or not a take–over bid should be referred to the Competition Commission.

OMX Index
Index of the Stockholm Stock Exchange.

On–exchange
Dealing of securities through a properly regulated investment exchange.

Open–outcry market
Dealing face to face on the floor of an exchange.

Order driven market
A stock market where brokers acting on behalf of clients match trades.

Ordinary Resolution
Resolution at a general meeting of a company which requires a 50% majority.

Ordinary shares
See *Equity shares.*

OTC
Over The Counter – dealing of securities outside of an organised exchange.

Paid in surplus
See *Share premium account*.

Panel on Take–overs and Mergers (PTM)
Non–statutory body which regulates the conduct of take–over offers. Responsible for the City Code.

Par value
See *Nominal value*.

Paying agent
A bank which handles payment of interest and dividends on behalf of the issuer of a security.

Payout ratio

$$\frac{\text{Dividend per share}}{\text{Earnings per share}} \times 100\%$$

PE ratio
See *Price earnings ratio*.

Penny share
A low priced and often speculative share.

Placing
A method of IPO by which shares are offered only to the clients of the issuing house.

plc
Public limited company (UK).

Pre–emption right
The right of shareholder whereby a company making a new issue of shares must offer the shares to the existing shareholders in proportion to their existing holdings.

Preference shares
Shares which are entitled to profits and assets in priority to the ordinary shares.

Preferred stock
See *Preference shares.*

Price earnings ratio
A ratio used by investors in shares. It is calculated as

$$\frac{\text{Market price per share}}{\text{Earnings per share}}$$

Primary market
The issuing of new securities to raise funds.

Private investor
An individual who holds securities solely for their own benefit.

Profit and loss account
Financial statement showing how the profit of the company has arisen over a period of time, usually a year, leading up to the bal-

ance sheet date. Under US reporting the profit and loss account is called the income statement.

Profit margin

$$\frac{\text{Profit}}{\text{Sales}} \times 100\%$$

Program trade
One of a number of trading strategies which involve the simultaneous purchase or sale of a number of different shares.

Prospectus
A formal document giving all relevant details about a new issue of shares – also called listing particulars.

PTM levy
A £1 levy on trades over £10,000 to help fund the Panel on Takeovers and Mergers.

Purple Book
See *Listing Rules.*

Quote driven market
A stock market where dealing is carried out with market makers.

Realised profit
Profit which has arisen from a real sale.

Record day
See *Books closed day.*

Registered share
A share where ownership is recorded on a register maintained by the issuer.

Registrar
The official with responsibility for maintaining the share register of a company.

Registrar of Companies
Official of the Department of Trade and Industry responsible for the formation and registration of companies and the general operation of Companies House.

Reserves of a company
The share premium account and the retained earnings of the company.

Retail Price Index
See *Consumer Price Index.*

Retained earnings
The accumulated retained profits, or earnings, of the company.

Return on assets
See *Return on capital employed.*

Return on capital employed
Other measurements are return on assets and return on equity.

Return on equity

See *Return on capital employed.*

Rights issue

A new issue of shares offered to the existing shareholders in proportion to their existing holdings.

Rolling settlement

A trade is settled a specified number of days after the date of the trade. Usually denoted as T+n where n is the number of business days. Thus T+3 means settlement 3 business days after the trade day.

Round lot

See *Board lot.*

Sale of rights nil paid

The sale of the entitlement to take up a rights issue – see also nil paid price.

Scrip dividend

A dividend paid in the form of additional shares in the company instead of cash

Scrip issue

An issue of new shares to existing shareholders in proportion to their existing shareholdings. Also called a bonus issue or capitalisation issue.

SEAQ

Stock Exchange Automated Quotation System –Computer system of the London Stock Exchange used by market makers to publish the prices they are quoting for share below the FTSE100, Shares on SEAQ have at least 2 market makers.

SEATS plus

Stock Exchange Alternative Trading Service – used for listed shares below the FTSE100 which have one or no market maker and for all AIM shares.

Second Section

The second tier market of the Tokyo Stock Exchange.

Secondary market

The trading of existing securities on an exchange.

SIS

Swiss central securities depository.

SETS

Stock Exchange Electronic Trading Service – A computerised order driven trading system for shares in the FTSE 100 and some other shares.

Settlement

The process whereby cash and ownership of a security are exchanged following a trade.

Share

The unit of ownership of a company.

Share buy back

Company purchases its own shares in the market and cancels them out – used as means of returning cash to shareholders.

Share capital

The figure in the balance sheet representing the nominal value of the shares that have been issued.

Share certificate

A certificate issued by a company to a shareholder stating either that a named person is the registered owner or that the bearer is the owner.

Share premium account

The figure in the balance sheet which represents the excess of the issue price of shares over the nominal value. USA accounts use the term 'paid in surplus'.

Share split or stock split

A split of a share into a number of shares with a smaller nominal value.

Shareholder

The owner of a share in a company – the part owner of a company.

Shareholders funds

Shows how the shareholders have funded the company through subscribing for capital and through the retention of profits. Shareholders funds is the total of the share capital and the reserves of the company.

Shareholders rights

The legal rights of a shareholder such as the right to vote at meetings.

Short selling

Selling of securities not owned by the seller.

Euroclear

Central securities depository for French corporate securities.

SIS

Swiss central securities depository.

Special Resolution

Resolution at a general meeting of a company which requires a 75% majority.

Specialist

A type of dealer on the New York Stock Exchange responsible for ensuring an orderly market in a small range of stocks.

Splitting rights

Splitting the entitlement to rights shares and selling some nil paid and subscribing for the remainder.

Sponsor
Firm which advises and helps a company obtain a listing.

Spread
The difference between the bid and offer prices.

Stag
An investor who applies for a new issue with a view to selling the shares at a handsome profit when the shares start trading in the secondary market.

Stamp Duty (UK)
Tax at the rate of $1/2\%$ payable on the purchase of UK equities in certificated form.

Stamp Duty Reserve Tax (SDRT) (UK)
Tax at the rate of $1/2\%$ payable on the purchase of UK equities in uncertificated form.

Standard and Poors 500
Index of the New York Stock Exchange.

Stock dividend
Another name for a scrip dividend.

Stock exchange
An organisation which provides facilities for companies and governments to issue securities to raise money and for those securities to be traded among investors.

Stockholder
See *Shareholder.*

Straits Times Index
Index of the Singapore Stock Exchange.

Subscription
The process of an investor paying for and taking up a new issue of shares.

T+n
Trade is settled n business days after the day of the trade. See *Rolling settlement.*

Technical analysis
Analysis of past share prices and making investment decisions on the basis of trends in those prices – see *Charts.*

Tick size
Minimum permitted movement in a share price.

Trade confirmation
Formal agreement of the details of a trade by the two counterparties prior to instructions being given for settlement. Often combined with trade matching.

Transparent
A description of a market where investors have full immediate knowledge of the details of trades taking place.

Two way price
The price at which a dealer is prepared to trade. It is quoted as separate bid and offer prices.

Unrealised profit
Profit which has not arisen from a sale – an increase in value of an asset.

Unweighted Index
Stock exchange index based solely on share prices – does not take into account the size of the companies.

virt-x
Stock exchange for trading UK listed equities and a wide range of European equities. It is in direct competition with the London Stock Exchange and is an alternative way of trading UK equities.

Weighted Index
Stock exchange index based on the market capitalisation of companies thus taking into account their sizes.

Winding up
See *Liquidation*.

Working capital
Net current assets.

XETRA
Dealing system of the Deutsche Börse.

AN INTRODUCTION TO EQUITY MARKETS

APPENDIX: USEFUL ADDRESSES

London Stock Exchange
Stock Exchange Tower
Old Broad Street
London EC2N 1HP
Tel: 020 7797 1000
Web: http://www.stockex.co.uk

CRESTCo Limited
33 Cannon Street
London EC4M 5SB
Tel: 020 7849 0000
Web: http://www.crestco.co.uk

Tradepoint Stock Exchange
35 King Street
London WC2E 8JD
Tel: 020 7240 8000
Web: http://www.tradepoint.co.uk

NASDAQ International
Durrant House
8-13 Chiswell Street
London EC1Y 4XY
Tel: 020 7374 6969
Web: http://www.nasdaq.com

Panel on Takeovers and Mergers
PO Box 226
The Stock Exchange Building
London EC2P 2JX
Tel: 020 7382 9026

Companies House
PO BOX 29019
21 Bloomsbury Street
London, WC1B 3XD
01222 380801
Web: http://www.companies-house.gov.uk/

Bank of England
Threadneedle Street
London EC2R 8AH
Tel: 020 7601 4444
Web: http://www.bankofengland.co.uk

Tokyo Stock Exchange
London Representative Office
4th Floor, Peninsular House
36 Monument Street
London EC3R 8LJ
Tel: 020 7236 0885
Web: http://www. tse.or.jp

Association of Private Client Investment Managers and Stockbrokers (APCIMS)
The Association was formed in 1990 to represent the interests of stockbroking firms which specialise in providing services for individual investors, or private clients as they are often known. Since its foundation APCIMS now represents well over 90% of private client stockbrokers and already a significant percentage of other investment managers.

112 Middlesex Street
London E1 7HY
Tel: 020 7247 7080
Website: http://www.moneyworld.co.uk/apcims

ProShare

ProShare is the leading organisation representing the interests of individual investors in the UK. Its objective is to promote share ownership for both private individuals and employees. Founded in 1992 as an independent, non-profit company limited by guarantee, it was initially funded by HM Treasury, The London Stock Exchange and twenty-two other companies. It is now funded by thousands of individual subscriptions, grants from charitable bodies and company sponsorship.

Library Chambers
13-14 Basinghall Street
London EC2V 5BQ
Tel: 020 7600 0984
Web: http://www.moneyworld.co.uk/investor

Financial Services Authority (FSA)

25 The North Colonnade
Canary Wharf
London E14 5HS
Tel: 020 7676 1000
Web: http://www.fsa.gov.uk

Securities and Futures Authority

Same address and telephone as the Financial services Authority

New York Stock Exchange
http://www.nyse.com

Deutsche Börse
http://www.exchange.de

Paris Bourse
http://www.bourse-de-paris.fr

EASDAQ
http://www.easdaq.be

AN INTRODUCTION TO EQUITY MARKETS

Securities Institute Publishing

Each publication provides a detailed overview and practical introduction to key topics within financial services.

Our range consists of re–worked and updated notes from our popular courses. These publications are a useful reference for everyone who needs to grasp the basics of a topic – fast!

To place an order or find out more, call now on *020 7645 0680.*

INTRODUCTION TO BOND MARKETS

Introduction to Bond Markets provides a comprehensive, authoritative description and analysis of the bond markets. The book considers basic 'plain vanilla' bonds and elementary bond mathematics, before looking at the array of different instruments available. Contents include:

- Bond Yield Measurement
- Corporate Debt Markets
- Eurobonds
- Introduction to Repo
- Risk Management
- Off–Balance Sheet Instruments
- Government Bond Markets
- Emerging Bond Markets.

410pp paperback, ISBN: 1 900520 79 6, 2nd edition

AN INTRODUCTION TO CORPORATE FINANCE
- Transactions and Techniques

Introduction to Corporate Finance provides readers with the key elements of corporate finance. The book introduces the principle techniques used in corporate finance, combined with practical experience and hands-on, numerically orientated case studies.

- Sources of Capital
- Flotations/Initial Public Offerings
- Mergers and Acquisitions
- Management Buy Outs
- Determining the Cost of Capital
- International Equity Offerings
- Valuing Securities
- Well illustrated with diagrams and tables, bullet points and summaries.

96pp paperback, ISBN: 1 900520 09 5

THE FUNDAMENTALS OF CREST

The Fundamentals of CREST gives a detailed overview of securities administration and settlement through the CREST system. It is illustrated throughout with diagrams and tables, bullet points and summaries.

■ Handling Certificated Securities
■ Corporate Actions and Claims
■ Stock Loans and Collateral.

128pp paperback, ISBN: 1 900520 98 2, 2nd edition

DICTIONARY OF FINANCIAL & SECURITIES TERMS

This updated and greatly expanded 2nd edition gives definitions of frequently used terms in the financial and securities industry. Also included is a comprehensive listing of abbreviations, acronyms and industry websites. Over 2,500 entries.

■ What is BIFFEX?
■ What does CDP stand for?
■ What are the Conduct of Business Rules?
■ What is the definition of Debt/Equity Ratio?

Included with the dictionary is a FREE CD–ROM version for users to load onto their PC for easy reference at home or at work.

400pp paperback, ISBN: 1 84307 023 5, 2nd edition

ECONOMIC & MONETARY UNION

Economic and Monetary Union (EMU) is the system that
links together the economies and currencies of the
participating European countries. The European Central
Bank has become responsible for centralised monetary
policy. What does the Euro mean for you?

- Convergence
- Impact of the Euro on the markets
- Preparing for the future.

28pp paperback, ISBN: 1 900520 31 1

INTRODUCTION TO EQUITY MARKETS

Introduction to Equity Markets provides an overview of
the current financial services industry. The book introduces
the reader to different types of companies and shares as
well as analysis of UK markets. An overview of dealing and
settlement in some of the world's major markets is also
featured. Contents include:

- Shareholders and Company Law
- Issuing Shares – The Primary Market
- Trading Shares – The Secondary Market
- Settlement of Transactions
- Major Overseas Exchanges and Indices
- Dividends, Bonus Issues and Rights Issues
- Company Accounts.

170pp paperback, ISBN: 1 84307 034 0, 2nd edition

AN INTRODUCTION TO FUND MANAGEMENT

An Introduction to Fund Management introduces readers to the economic rationale for the existence of funds, the different types available, investment strategies and many other related issues from the perspective of the investment manager. Topics include the features and characteristics of funds, portfolio management and administration, performance measurement and investment mathematics. Includes relevant formulae, equations and examples.

- Features and characteristics of funds
- Portfolio management and administration
- Performance measurement
- Investment mathematics.

160pp paperback, ISBN: 1 84307 022 7, 2nd edition

FUNDAMENTALS OF GLOBAL OPERATIONS MANAGEMENT

This book will help you to understand the role of operations terms and what is happening in the industry that impacts on operations. It is ideal for anyone new to or aspiring to become a supervisor or manager.Contents include:

- Operations management
- Markets
- Banking, broking and institutional clients
- Concepts of risk
- Clearing and settlement
- Custody
- Technology
- Regulation and compliance

272pp paperback, ISBN: 1 84307 014 6

INTRODUCTION TO THE GILT STRIPS MARKET

Introduction to the Gilt Strips Market provides a thorough description and analysis of gilt strips. The contents describe and define strips as a financial instrument and examine the use and application of gilt strips within the context of the capital markets as a whole. Contents include:

- Zero–coupon bonds
- The yield curve
- Interest rate risk for strips
- Settlement, tax and regulatory issues
- Trading and strategy

192pp paperback, ISBN: 1 84307 006 5, 2nd edition

THE PREVENTION OF MONEY LAUNDERING

This quick guide looks at the scale of the problem and efforts taken to overcome it: an essential reference for all who are concerned to identify attempts at money laundering within their organisation.

- What is money laundering?
- Money laundering and the law
- How do you spot it in the process, and what to do.

48pp paperback, ISBN: 1 84307 005 7, 2nd edition

UNDERSTANDING REGULATION AND COMPLIANCE

Understanding Regulation & Compliance outlines the new regulatory structure in the post-N2 environment, introducing the areas regulated under the *Financial Services and Markets Act 2000*, the role of the *Financial Services Authority* and the rules imposed on firms. It also introduces other important regulatory areas such as *Insider Dealing and Money Laundering*. Topics include:

- Financial Services & Markets Act 2000
- Financial Services Authority
- FSA Handbook
- Control over individuals
- Conduct of business rules
- Client assets
- Improper dealings
- Money laundering

192pp paperback, ISBN: 1 84307 003 2, 2nd edition

INTRODUCTION TO REPO MARKETS

An Introduction to Repo Markets provides a comprehensive description and analysis of the repo markets. The text has been written to cater for those with little or no previous experience of the repo markets, though it also develops the subject matter to sufficient depth to be of use to more experienced practitioners. Contents include:

- Uses and economic functions of repo
- Accounting, Tax and Capital issues
- The UK gilt repo market
- The implied repo rate and basis trading
- Repo and the yield curve

240pp paperback, ISBN: 1 900520 86 9 2nd edition

AN INTRODUCTION TO SWAPS

An Introduction to Swaps gives a detailed overview of how the various categories of swap work, how they are traded and what they are used for. Topics include interest rate swaps, managing risk, asset swaps, currency swaps. The book is illustrated with over 50 diagrams and tables.

- Managing risk with swaps
- Asset swaps
- Currency swaps.

160pp paperback, ISBN: 1 900520 21 4

AN INTRODUCTION TO VALUE–AT–RISK

An Introduction to Value–at–Risk has been written for those with little or no previous understanding of or exposure to the concepts of risk management and Value–at–Risk. Topics include applications of VaR, instrument structures, stress testing, VaR for corporates, credit risk and legal/regulatory issues.

- Risk and Risk management
- VaR and Derivatives, Fixed Interest products.
- VaR for Corporates

208pp paperback, ISBN: 1 84307 035 9, 3rd edition

SECURITIES INSTITUTE PUBLISHING

For further details on these and other new titles, contact our Client Services Department on 020 7645 0680

Forthcoming titles

Retail Publications
- Advanced Operations Management
- Futures, Options and Other Derivatives Products
- Products, Trading and Operations
- Custody, Stock Lending and Derivatives Clearing
- Risk Management
- Clearing Settlement and Custody Operations
- Products and Trading from an Operations Perspective
- Mutual Funds

Securities Institute/Butterworth-Heinemann Global Capital Markets Series
- IPO and Equity Offerings
- Controls, Procedures and Risk
- Clearing, Settlement and Custody
- Managing Technology in the Operations Function
- Relationship and Resource Management in Operations
- Understanding the Markets
- Credit Risk

For further information on this series please call *01865 888180* or visit http://www.bh.com/finance/

We plan to introduce new titles into our retail range in the forthcoming year. All the titles listed are provisional and may be subject to alteration.